LOCKED IN NUMBERS

"The Driving Force Of My Obsessive Compulsive Disorder"

Jeffrey Benson

ISBN-13: 9780578306247

Cover design by: Jeffrey Benson
Library of Congress Registration Number: TXu 2-267-652
Printed in the United States of America

I dedicate my book to all of the souls that live through each and every day and suffer through the pain of living with and dealing with having the Obsessive Compulsive Disorder. My heart goes out to them as well as their parents who have had to watch their children bearing / suffering with the emotional and physical pain of a life with OCD. These caring parents love us enough to be a part of our lives and help us, talk to us, and be there for us any way that they can. Their dedication and love is what keeps us strong and powerful and gives us the ability to survive!

I especially want to thank my own Mother for her "Never Give Up!" attitude. My Mother, without all current information about this disorder always knew that there was something not quite right with her son. Her dedication, love and strength in my life has truly made me the man I am today and for that, I am forever grateful.

BE STRONG AND NEVER GIVE UP!

CONTENTS

CHAPTER 1: A LITTLE ABOUT MYSELF!

"How I Discovered That I Had Obsessive Compulsive Disorder"

L et me start by telling you a little about myself. The starting point is my childhood. This is the time that I did not know that I had Obsessive Compulsive Disorder (henceforth OCD). This is also the overall process that I went through in order to be properly diagnosed with OCD. I will also include the process that my Mother went through in order to get to my real issue. There was a lot of trial and error that occurred in order to figure out what was wrong. This included the focus on some of my odd behavior. There were many different visits to many different doctors and neurologists. My Mother was relentless in her pursuit of the truth. She spoke to me on many different occasions in order to sort of "Self-Diagnose" the issue. It is also important to note that this was during the early 1970's and 1980's. The reason that this is so important to mention is because we did not have the technology that we have today. There was no internet, cell phones, iPads, tablets, PC's or Macs. Some of the technology did exist, but it was not in the hands of the average consumer. There were no Apple stores, online ordering, internet searching, texting, emails, GPS on phones and in cars. There was no way to just press a few buttons on your phone and have a couch, shovel and pet food delivered directly to your door in a few days. Imagine that while driving, you actually had to know how to get to where you were going without the help of a GPS hooked up to a satellite guiding your every turn. Get this, kids used to actually go outside! We played games and rode bicycles to nearby pizza places. We did not play a virtual reality game where we are "Riding" a bicycle. Pretty weird, right? Every child from age one and up did not have the technology they do now. Children did not have a room filled with high tech gaming systems. Children did not have wide screen TV's that were hooked up to the newest technology that allowed them to communicate with other people all over the world that were all playing the same game through a headset. Every child did not have their own, or even know how to use, their own cell phone, iPad, laptop, tablet; loaded with their favorite games and applications. The point is that the world was VERY different then.

The point of bringing up the difference in times is because there was no internet where we could just find a search engine. There was no way to just type in your symptoms. The reliance was on printed matter where you had to know exactly what you were looking for. You could not simply sit for one-one millionth (if that's even a real word) of a second while page after page loads onto the screen with answers to your inquiry appearing from all over the earth. There were no media sites where you could scroll through symptoms and see what they were connected to. There were no articles where you could find that a famous doctor had written and described each symptom. There were absolutely no blogs where people with OCD described their symptoms and you or your parents could match them up with yourself or your child. There was no way to ask or post a question and get an answer quickly. Basically, there was no way to discuss your situation with the millions of people all over the world that shared your experience. The bottom line was, if you wanted or needed any sort of information at all, you were EXTREMELY limited to say the least. You would have to use the local resources that were around you. You could watch a news special, read a magazine, a book or actually talk to another human being. Weird right? In fact, this is how my Mother figured out that I had Tourette's Syndrome. She read about it in a magazine at a doctor's office.

Interesting right? It is hard to believe that people used to read actual words printed on paper and not on a cell phone, computer screen, laptop, tablet or watch. But a trip to a neurologist confirmed it. It showed up as tics and arm and leg spasms. At this point in time, it was not
known that Tourette's Syndrome was under the OCD umbrella. Both of these disorders are genetic. My Mother then recognized the signs in my paternal Grandfather and he told her that my Father had the same tics since childhood but hid them well. My Father had been silent all this time.

Tourette's Syndrome is just another fun item that you get with the OCD package. It comes free of charge. For the purpose of this book, I focus on the OCD side of things. This is because it is the major issue that I deal with on a day to day basis. The Tourette's Syndrome has an effect, but does not waste a ton of time in my day to day life. You can research Tourette's Syndrome like anything else. Please feel free to do just that. Anyway, let me get back to my childhood.

Our story starts off in a faraway place with a magical forest! Alright, that is a complete falsehood. I just thought it sounded more interesting and dramatic. The truth is that I grew up in Los Angeles. Not as exciting, but true. I grew up in a normal house in a small suburban neighborhood. There were several families in my neighborhood.

I had a lot of friends that lived very close to my home. Most of my friends lived right down the street. I used to hang out with these kids every afternoon. It was a lot of fun. I would go to their house or they would come over to mine. We all could meet somewhere and play in the street or in someone's back yard. We rode bicycles, tossed a ball around, played basketball or went swimming. There were tons of birthdays to celebrate. We would usually have a parent BBQ with hamburgers and hotdogs. Neighborhood families would come over. We would swim and eat. It would all end with a special dessert. My friends and I also spent a lot of time at a local mall. It was a few blocks away. We went to the arcades, ate fast food and went to candy stores. It was a fun time in my life. I walked to school and back. It was only a few blocks from my house. It was a time where there would be kids playing in the street. They would all know each other and do stuff together. It was when parents did not have to worry as the neighborhood was safe. It was a calm and quiet area with tons of families. The basic point is that I had a very normal childhood.

My immediate family was my Mother and Father who have since divorced and an older Sister who has since given me two fabulous Nephews. My Father worked at a movie studio. This was so interesting as we were able to see firsthand what it was like to make movies. We would walk around the studio lot and in and out of the sound stages. We were able to see the sets of all of the movies that were currently in production. It was very exciting. I also had Aunts and Uncles and cousins who came to visit.

The OCD started to show up around the age of eight. I started to do some odd things. Nothing major, just a few different things. I felt that I needed to pet the cat four times. I needed to do things a certain way. There were things that I had to touch or look at a certain way.

My Mother observed these things. She noticed these things that I was doing. She realized that they were not the normal childlike things to do. I would look at my matchbox cars differently and a certain number of times. I would think differently than most people. I would have different reactions to things. She noticed that I was having a lot of trouble in school. Especially with paying attention and doing the homework. She made sure that I always had tutors and people to help me complete my school work.

She took me to a bunch of doctors as a child. We were at a different doctor every few months. We saw many different therapists and neurologists. I was diagnosed with everything from having too much sugar to other ridiculous theories. Each doctor mentioned a new and different thing that they thought that I could be suffering from. The overall issue was that they all had a lot to say about nothing. They all tried to figure me out. Each one had a different theory as to what it might be. There was the theory that karate would help. It did not. There was the theory that I needed to eat more natural foods. It did not help. There were tons and tons of theories that were just not validated. My Mother even went to a hospital to ask questions. The nurse there told her that she was just an overly nervous Mother. So much for that one.

One day my Mother was in a doctor's office. She started to read a pamphlet on OCD and the symptoms involved. That was her AHA! moment. She finally figured it out. She said to herself "That is what he has!". Ever since then, we knew. We now had our golden answer. I had OCD. I was eleven years old then and relieved to know that what I had was not my "fault".

Once we had the answer, the research became different. My Mother started to research the different things that were out there and what they would help. We did not think of any sort of drugs as I was too young. They were all things like getting more exercise or help to do better in school.

My childhood went on and I began to get used to the OCD. I did not worry about it. It was not too strong and the symptoms were not horrible. There were not too many of them. I had my quirks. The major issue was counting. The symptoms slowly started to grow. I began checking. My Mother would kiss me goodbye as I went off to school. I repeated to her to double check to make sure that there was no lipstick on my face. I checked over and over to make sure that I had my house keys. I also checked to make sure that I brought the correct books to school.

I began to get good at the hiding aspect of it. None of my friends even knew that I had anything at all. I was good at hiding these things. I started to develop other little issues over time.

CHAPTER 2: THE EXPLOSION!

"The Year My Life Changed!"

My life was pretty normal prior to turning twenty-two years old. I had a life just like everyone else at that age. I hung out with my friends and stayed out late. I had my entire life ahead of me. I did not realize how lucky I was. I could do anything I wanted to do and had every option known to man. This included any career option. I could travel or live anywhere in the world.

My OCD was very low. I did not realize how low that it actually was. It was basically nothing. I did some counting, checking and repeating. I did have a few obsessions, but they were minimal at best. At the time, I thought that the OCD was bad here and there. I had no idea that what I thought was bad was absolutely nothing. I had pretty low tone symptoms.

I turned twenty-two and my life literally changed forever. The OCD literally EXPLODED on me. It got instantly horrific. I had no idea what had happened. It had completely changed and was relentless.

The symptoms that I had were increasingly worse. The checking was the highest that I have ever seen in the numbers required. The repeating was nonstop. The thoughts ran wild. I literally could not keep up with the OCD. It was all over me. It felt like someone had put an OCD blanket over me and I was smothered underneath it.

There were a whole bunch of new symptoms that began. These were symptoms that I had never known prior to this explosion. These new symptoms were awful and painful. The thoughts I had, lingered for days. And anxiety showed up.

I had no idea what anxiety was before the explosion. The anxiety was at a high level all the time. It was paralyzing. The anxiety skyrocketed on every single issue and lingered for a long time just like the thoughts. It was very hard to fight it.

I really thought that I knew OCD when I really had no clue. After the explosion, I felt as if I was learning what OCD was for the very first time. The OCD began the second I woke up and lasted until I went to sleep. It was always at a high level. It was intertwined in everything that I did. I could not even brush my teeth without it being there.

The OCD had me locked down completely. It was a very depressing time. I had no idea what had happened. My life changed overnight. I had no idea what to do. I had to just struggle through it.

After a few months I was sort of able to navigate through the stronger OCD symptoms. It took a little while to get used to it. I struggled to try my best. It was not an easy task by any means.

I needed some help to deal with it. I went to a behavioral therapist. He taught me ways to deal with the OCD. He trained me on Cognitive Behavior Therapy (CBT). It seemed to work for a little while but not perfectly. It was a constant battle to sustain the CBT when the OCD was raging.

I was not on any formal medication so I did not have the help of a pharmaceutical. I had to do the CBT cold turkey. It was very hard. It really needs medication to back it up. The medication provides a sort of foundation for the behavior therapy.

It was a very hard time in my life. I could not assimilate what had happened. I tried to distract myself over and over. It did not work. It was just too hard to deal with. I really had a problem and needed more help. To this day, I do not know whether it got better or I just got stronger.

I tried a few homeopathic products that were designed to calm someone down. They were designed to make you relax. They were made to induce a calming feeling. This was not the case. The OCD was just too strong. The supplements were not able to help me. I was completely depressed. The OCD was like a runaway train. My life had changed forever.

CHAPTER 3: OBSESSIONS AND COMPULSIONS!

"After All, It's The Thought That Counts!"

"Obsessive" is the beginning of the title of the disorder as these thoughts start the cycle. There are millions of ways that the medical community could formally define an obsession. The online community would define it another way. The high level neurologists have their own definition. I am also sure that there are millions of books that have great descriptive explanations and terms to describe an obsession. I have heard a lot of the terms and most of them are described as "Irrational Thoughts". This is a thought that is not real or possible. I have heard the term "Unwanted". This is a thought that is something you don't want to think about.

I have had OCD for over forty years. Basically, I have done a lot of research. I would define an obsession as "Forced". The thought is always annoying because it is intrusive and it makes no sense. There are two different reasons for this. One, the fact that it happened at all. Two, the fact that you will need to do a few things to end it. The thought materializes instantly. That INSTANT is when you know that you will need to either complete "Compulsive" behavior or sit through it by not doing anything. Either way is terrible.

I would say that there are three types of obsessions because there are three basic scenarios that occur. Each of these scenarios are separate and different in nature. They all require a compulsion. The difference is the overall reason for the compulsion. The point being: you do the compulsion either way.

The obsession is the beginning of everything. The obsession starts it all. It is the beginning of the entire process. It is the "Meat" of the OCD. For the vegetarians, I guess it is the "Avocado" or the "Tofu" of the OCD. Anyway, you get the point. Maybe that's why it comes first in the title. I also think Compulsive Obsessive Disorder does not sound as good. The reality is that the type of obsession does not matter. The only thing that matters is that the obsession occurs.

The first type of obsession is the irrational thought. This is exactly what it sounds like. It is usually something impossible or improbable in nature. The amount of irrational thoughts that a person can have are unlimited. Nothing is more creative than your own mind. The key word is irrational. You know it is irrational the second you get it. This is a type of obsession that most people with OCD have to deal with. The reality is that we all do not have the same irrational thoughts. But it could be that some people may share the same irrational thought. I am sure that there is or should be a top ten list for obsessions. I am not sure if the medical community even has a clue as to why each person has different thoughts. I don't think they even care. I think they are just trying to cure OCD as a whole. They don't care about the little nuts and bolts that make up each thought. I also think it is because they don't know what causes these thoughts. This would make it a moving target. It would be almost impossible to try and come out with a different medication for each thought. It would never work. Needless to say, the medical community just tries to blanket all of the symptoms under the name of OCD. This is why the medications are not good. They try to fix everything with one magic pill. There is no such panacea. This is how the medical community spreads themselves thin. It is too bad.

An irrational thought can be anything under the sun. Feel free to get creative with this one. They are triggered just like every other obsession. They can involve everything from having Cancer to your car being stolen. These thoughts can be very ridiculous. They make no sense whatsoever. I guess that's why they are called irrational. I still prefer the technical term of "Baloney".

Here is an example of what an irrational thought is like: Imagine you are parking your car. You turn the car off and get out. You hit the alarm button to automatically lock the car door. You hear the beep. The OCD immediately kicks in. You now feel that you need to hit the button and relock the car three times. The obsession is that if you do not do the compulsion and lock the car all three times, it will be stolen. If you walk away and don't do it; it will just get worse. The anxiety and thought will just strengthen. The feeling is that your car will be stolen. You might even get a visual of people stealing your car or you coming back out to a parking space with broken window glass and no car. This is why it is an irrational thought. Let's face it, if your car is going to get stolen, it does not matter how many times you lock it. I really doubt criminals are waiting in a parking lot watching with binoculars; looking to see if someone did not lock their car three times. The other reality is that if someone is going to steal your car, they will not simply walk up to your car and look in and say: "Hey, this car has been locked three times so forget it". Then just move on. This is why I call them baloney. The fact that your car may or may not get stolen or broken into will not change depending on how many times you did or did not lock it. By doing the compulsion, you are not protecting your car any more. That is the point of this particular irrational thought. It does not matter how many times you check your car. This logic is impossible. In fact, it is not logic at all. If you check the car three times, your car will not be stolen. If you check it two or four times, it will be stolen. The reason this is nonsense is due to the fact that if you check the car correctly, such as three times, it still might get stolen. If you don't check it correctly, such as two or four times, the car might be perfectly safe and never have a problem. I think of this thought as a macro thought because something simple develops into a whole story that is not real.

Here is another example of an irrational thought: Let's say that you are home and it's a weekend. You make your morning coffee. You pour it into a cup. You like cream in your coffee. So, you open up the refrigerator and take out the cream. You pour a little into your coffee and put it back in the refrigerator. You close the refrigerator door. The OCD strikes. You immediately get a thought that you need to close the refrigerator door the right number of times. If your number is seven. It needs to be closed seven times. If you do not do the refrigerator door compulsion, you will receive a call from a relative. The relative went to the doctor and has Cancer. If you do the compulsion, you will not get a call because your relative or loved one will be completely healthy and fine. Once again, the reality is that your loved one's health does not change depending on whether or not you close the refrigerator door seven times. The refrigerator has absolutely no effect on anyone's health. Just like with the car being stolen. If you have a relative that is a Cancer patient, it is definitely not because you did not do the compulsion. The truth is that it really does not matter how many times you open and close your refrigerator for cream. The fridge is not magical and has no effect on anything. A human's fate does not depend on home food cooling devices. It is just an appliance and nothing more.

Yet another example: Let's say you are shopping in a supermarket. You are looking for potato chips. You find the aisle, brand and flavor you like. There are a bunch of bags on the shelf. All are the exact same flavor. You grab one off of the shelf. BOOM!!! The obsessive thought hits. The bag you just grabbed is not good. You have a thought that if you choose that particular bag, you will change the course of your life. Your life will be somehow different. If you take that bag, you will lose your job. Your house might burn down. Your life will be ruined somehow. So, naturally, you put that bag back on the shelf and grab another one. A second goes by and the thought shows up again. The same thought attaches itself to the new bag. So, as usual, you grab another bag. This time, the thought does not happen. The bag is safe. Your life will remain safe and prosperous. That is the bag you decide to take. Now, as we have been discussing. This is completely irrational, impossible and baloney. There is absolutely no possible way a bag of potato chips has that kind of power. If this were true, you would not go to Church or Temple. You would just go to aisle six of the market. There you would find Tibetan Monks praying to a bag of cool ranch flavored potato chips. Maybe they would argue as to whether the Universe speaks through the bacon flavor or the sea salt and vinegar. The truth is that this is complete nonsense. The thought that one of the two identical bag of chips is somehow different is truly impossible. They are both made out of the same bag material. Made in the same factory. Made with the same factory machine. They are the exact same product. Sure, there may have been a problem in the factory and the bags might have a different amount of chips in them or one is ripped. But other than those tiny differences, that's it. After all, they are both JUST BAGS OF CHIPS! Everyone else in the world just buys them, eats them and throws the bag away. But, for those of us with OCD, it's just not that easy. The fact is that these thoughts haunt us. The reality is that there is no such possibility of your life changing due to the bag of chips you bought. You will not win the lottery and become a millionaire because you bought one bag of chips instead of another. On the other hand, if you do lose your job, it is also not due to which bag of chips that you bought that day. If that were true, people would spend their lives finding the "Right" bag of chips so that they will have a great life. On the other hand, if you meet someone going through a hard time in their life, they would blame the bag of chips that they bought the week before. It is just impossible and not true. The thought is exactly what it is, an irrational lie. Chips have absolutely no power on someone's life one way or another....PERIOD!

To sum up irrational thoughts or obsessions with one word: "Unreal". They are basically thought garbage. They are not true and usually impossible. The irrational thoughts are just something to invoke a negative emotion such as fear. They are usually something that will scare you. They are designed to make the OCD sufferer scared or afraid of the thought. This is why they are always scary in nature. They only exist to scare the person having them. There are many different types of irrational thoughts. They can happen whenever or wherever. The key to remember is that ninety percent of them are scary. They are usually something that the OCD sufferer is afraid of happening or being true. Something that you do not want to happen. Something that will make you depressed, sad or in pain if it actually did happen. Always a bad thing. Once in a while, you might have one that is a good thing, but most of the time, they are not. They range from things that you have touched, moved, said, felt, etc. They could be out of the blue i.e. a completely new thought that you have never had before. They consist of subjects that trigger a fear. Think of the example of the bags of potato chips. Imagine the stress you would be under if you felt that your entire life would fall apart depending on the bag of chips that you bought. How about this? What if you felt that the Devil/Evil/Negativity will come after you; depending on the bag of chips that you buy. Not as fun, right? These irrational thoughts can also include such things as your spouse leaving you, you having health problems, you having car trouble, your loved one getting a disease, you losing your job, you never meeting the right person to marry, you not up for a promotion, you killing someone, your best friends hating you, you ruining something, you causing pain to someone, you embarrassing yourself, your house getting broken into, you hurting a baby, you getting Cancer, ad infinitum. The bottom line is that it is usually something scary. It is usually pure fantasy but can include sprinkles of something possible or real. The hard truth of the irrational form of obsession is that it is not related to reality. Now you know or have learned about obsessive irrational thoughts.

The second type of obsession is what I would call a "Real"

or "Normal" obsession. These real / normal thoughts are the opposite of the irrational thoughts or obsessions. The reason I call them "Real" or "Normal" is because, unlike the irrational thoughts, these thoughts are actually possible. They usually occur with the mundane day to day events such as paying bills, checking off errands, making sure you got everything done that you needed to, etc. They can always occur during social events as a sort of check point or review of how you functioned during the social event. The can be started by a call to a friend or a family member or a business. They occur during and after conversations with people or events that happen. They might happen due to the fear or the stress of something that you may have said incorrectly to someone. The bottom line is that they are normal thoughts. Most people have these thoughts or feelings every day. The difference with someone with OCD is that the obsessive brain keeps the thought or "Obsesses" on each thought. Most people who have these thoughts or feelings usually have them, thing nothing of them, conclude something about them, etc. They are usually a quick thought and they are over in seconds. Never to return. The person simply forgets about them. Maybe they have some small reaction to it. The thought is gone just as fast as it comes. Someone with OCD, on the other hand, will continue to think about this little thought ad nauseam. The thought simply does not end or fade. These normal thoughts or feelings linger for a few hours. Sometimes they can last a few days or weeks. They sometimes re-occur weeks later. They usually come with a compulsion in order to end them. They linger until the compulsion is completed. The compulsion usually involves some form of repeating and/or checking. The idea being that the compulsion usually gets rid of the thought or, at least, lowers the power of the thought. It also lowers the accompanying anxiety. The repeating or checking compulsion starts. If you begin to do the compulsion, numbers and sets begin. Then the compulsion becomes to repeat it the correct number of times, the correct number of sets and in the correct number of places. The thought persists and persists. It does not go away until the repeating or

confirming is done and all sets are completed. (This process ap-
plies to irrational thoughts as well.) The thought might be bad
enough that it still lingers even after the numbers are done. This
usually ends up in a multi-day compulsion. These normal obsessions can blow up and be completely out of control. These can
often occur if the thought has a feeling of nervousness, fear, sadness, anger or some other emotion attached. The stronger the
emotion is, the stronger the thought is. The stronger the
thought is, the stronger the compulsion is. This can lead to very
high anxiety. The higher the anxiety, the higher the numbers
and sets are.

The emotion can be fear. Maybe you are afraid that you
embarrassed yourself somewhere. Maybe you are afraid that you
insulted someone during a professional dinner party. Maybe you
are angry at something someone said to offend you at the dinner
party. The fear might exist on a small note if you feel you made
a mistake. Maybe you paid a bill late and you are afraid that the
company will turn off your service. Maybe you are worried that
your healthcare or car insurance will be canceled. The higher
the emotion, the worse the thought is. Like I mentioned earlier,
everyone goes through this in life. Everyone has these thoughts
and feelings. They are a part of everyday life. They are perfectly
normal and usual for people to have. The difference with someone with OCD is that these thoughts will linger and grow into a
major OCD storm that might last for days. Remember, these are
normal everyday thoughts that are possible and can actually be
true.

Here is an example of a normal obsession: Let's say you are
at a dinner party. You know some of the people but not all. Some
are good friends and others you just met that night. Everyone
is sitting around the dinner table with glasses of wine. A few
minutes go by and the host brings out a tray of freshly baked
cookies. Everyone grabs a cookie to taste it. Someone asks "What
do you think, Jeff?". I know most of the people there. They all
know that I have a sense of humor. I quickly reply "They are

crap and should be thrown away!". My friends know that I was joking. One of them tells everyone that Jennifer made them. She is one of the people sitting at the table. She is new to the crowd so I don't really know her. She laughs at my joke. I then mention how great they are. She says thank you. I ask Jennifer if they were hard to make. The conversation continues from there. A few minutes go by and I wonder if I offended her by saying the cookies were horrible? I hope she knew that I was kidding. I hope she knew that I really did like them. Now remember the reality. Everyone laughed knowing it was a joke. Jennifer, herself, laughed knowing that it was a joke. I also told her that I loved them and that they were great. We had an entire conversation over them. But the OCD thought still occurs. It is now an official thought. I am still at the dinner party so I am busy enough with the conversation to put the thought aside for now. The truth is that the thought is not too strong. But it still exists. I am now sitting at a dinner party with a thought that is not even true. I start to think of the thought instead of having fun with my friends which is the whole point of going to a dinner party with friends in the first place. As I look around the table I see everyone talking, drinking, eating cookies and, more importantly, laughing. No thoughts. No anxiety. No repeating.

Then there is me. I am sitting there with a plastic smile on my face having to focus on two things. One, the conversation with friends. Two, the thought that I offended Jennifer. All this instead of having fun with my friends. I get up to go to the bathroom. In the bathroom, I repeat to myself. "I did not offend Jennifer. She knew it was a joke.". I leave the bathroom and rejoin the dinner party. An hour or so goes by and the dinner party ends. We all make a few last jokes, plan to have another dinner party and say goodbye to each other. I know that my night is not over without some friendly repeating.

I get into my car and just sit there. I repeat "I did not offend Jennifer. She knew my comment on the cookies was a joke.". Then, as usual, the thought changes and grows a little. I now have a thought that I made a fool of myself or embarrassed my-self in front of my own friends. So, let's add that to the repeating. "I did not offend Jennifer. She knew my comment on the cookies was a joke. I did not make a fool of myself.". Now remember, my numbers are three and five. There are three sentences there. I will add two more to make it a clean five. I make sure that I am keeping track of the repeating numbers and sets correctly. I am doing my usual which is counting on my hands where each finger is a number. So, for the purpose of this example. Let's count them out. Number one (Finger One): "I did not offend Jennifer.". Number two (Finger two): "She knew my comment on the cookies was a joke.". Number three (Finger Three): "I did not make a fool of myself.". Let's add two more to make it a full five count. Number Four (Finger Four): "The conversation went fine.". Number Five (Finger Five): " Everything went fine tonight.". I add a "Done!" to close or complete the set. That was one complete set. I immediately feel as if I did not say anything. I was quietly sitting in the car. I feel that I did not say the five things while counting on my fingers. I need to repeat this entire sequence four more times to complete five sets. "Done!", "Done!", "Done!", "Done!", "Done!".

I am now driving home. I pull my car into the parking space, turn it off and get out. I slam my door and beep it three times. I check to make sure the headlights are off three times. This is a normal thought that if my lights are on, they may shine into someone's house and annoy them or my car battery will die and I will need to call AAA in the morning. Anyway, if you remember, I repeated about Jennifer's cookies in two places. The house where the dinner party was held and the car before I drove home. I now need to do it in three other places to make it a com-plete set of five sets. I will not bore you by making you have to re-read it. Just know it is the same.

So, I do the same thing as before including counting on my fingers. I do a quick set on the way to my house. This is three places which are the house, the car and outside on the way to the house. I need to add two more places. I go into the house and do a quick set. I grab my garbage as an excuse to leave again. Hey I might as well get some housework done while repeating my guts out, right. So, I go outside to the garbage and do a quick set outside. This is now five sets of five places.

Now the OCD changes. I did all of the repeating compulsions the way they should be done. I now feel as if the five sets of five places are one set of five. So, I need to either do it another set of five places or maybe even five more sets of five places. Just a quick note, if each set is a total of twenty-five, then five giant sets would mean that I need to repeat a total of one hundred and twenty five times. All over a cookie that I had at a dinner party instead of having fun. Trust me. There is no cookie that good. I decide that I am not going to do it. I am too tired. I will just go to bed and do another set of five sets tomorrow.

So, we are now into day two of the cookie repeating. I get up in the morning and feel I need to finish the cookie sets. I get up and do another five sets of five hand counting and all. All of this over a dinner party that was supposed to be fun and a cookie that was not even that great. Get how the OCD works?

Here is why I labeled the cookie thought a normal or real obsession. The thought is based on something realistic. The truth is that the dinner party was the first time I ever met Jennifer. I don't know her. I don't know what she is like. I don't know her life at all. She also does not know me or anything about me. She does not know that I have a sense of humor at all. The truth of the matter is that she may have been offended by my first comment where I mentioned that the cookies were not good. I might have actually made her unhappy. It is very possible that I could have offended someone with a comment like that. Maybe she is the type of person that is very proud of her baking skills. You never know. Maybe she was just laughing to be nice in a social situation. I really doubt that I made a fool of myself with that comment. But, this is also possible.

Now, the reality of the situation is that Jennifer laughed because she knew that it was a joke. She got the joke. She knew I was just kidding. I saw her laugh and react to the whole thing. I also saw my friends laugh so I know that I did not embarrass myself. The dinner party obviously went fine. There was no issue to be concerned with no matter what. I also want to add that if Jennifer did get offended by that little comment, who cares. That's her problem if she does not have a sense of humor. Either way, what do I care? I might never see her again. The truth is that even if she was offended, it would not have been for long. I am sure that she would have just said "Whatever" and moved on completely forgetting about the comment.

Now, let's cover the reality about the entire situation. The truth is that this is a real and possible thought. Jennifer laughing should have told you that it was fine. Your friends laughing should have told you that you did not embarrass yourself. This should be enough for most people to move on with their night and completely forget the event. No harm. No foul. The truth is that I just went to a dinner party and made jokes like everyone else...PERIOD...END OF STORY....

The OCD takes this normal thought and runs with it. It lingers in your head for a long period of time. You need to repeat about it in the sets of numbers in or to feel that it is over and went fine.

The reality is that people can make fools of themselves in social situations. You see why I refer to these lingering thoughts as a normal or a real thought? They are possible and based on a reality. They are a thought that the entire world could have. The OCD then takes it and blows it completely out of proportion. There are emotions attached where you feel fearful, worried or anxious that you made a mistake in a social situation. It is upsetting. This fuels the OCD. The OCD then takes it and blows it completely out of proportion. Makes it into a huge deal. You feel like it is the worst thing you have ever done. You really screwed up. You start to believe it depending on the amount of anxiety you have. You are feeding the thought. It explodes into a complete pile of crap. It makes the entire situation stressful and uncomfortable. It also does not help that you know the reality is that all the people at the dinner party had fun. They all just went home like a normal night. It was just a dinner party to them. To someone with OCD, it is an entire night of stress, counting, repeating, etc. An entire OCD storm. After all, you just wanted to have a little fun with some friends.

How about another example: Let's say I am talking on the phone to a good friend. John and I have been friends for a long time. We are discussing our jobs. John says "Why don't you get a real job?". All of a sudden, I get anxiety. I feel insulted. John basically inadvertently insults me. That triggers a quick and small burst of anxiety. I do not want to confront John so I just let it go. The conversation flows from there. A few minutes later, we both hang up.

Now, you know me and the OCD system by now. So, is it over? Nope! I get mad that John insulted me. This triggers the feeling of anger. The anger triggers anxiety. The anxiety triggers the OCD. So, I start out with trying to blow it off. I say "Fuck John. He's an idiot." Just like with the dinner party in the previous example. The anger, anxiety and the thought lingers. I feel that I need to repeat: "Fuck John. He's an idiot." again. Then the numbers start. The OCD takes it and runs. It is now a full blown OCD storm. It grows and grows into repeating over and over. "Fuck John. He's an idiot.". This goes on and on. I keep trying to blow it off and the thought still lingers. The anger and anxiety kicks up here and there during the day. This strengthens the thought. I end up doing a compulsion. This ends up just like the cookie obsession. I end up doing it five sets of five in five different places. Very tiring. This also lasts for the full two days.

The reason I classify this as a normal thought or real obsession is because it is a realistic thought. It is very normal to get angry when someone insults you. It is a human response. Even if John is an asshole, it still makes you mad. When you are mad, the thought lingers. The thought lingers so the repeating grows and continues. The anger returns every time I think of my friend John or our conversation. This might last a few days or return in a few weeks or months. The return might trigger compulsions. It does not always happen. If it does, the lingering thoughts and compulsions are not as strong as they were when they first hit. The bottom line is that my getting mad was a normal human reaction to John's comment. He insulted me without knowing it. I got mad just like everyone else would. The difference is with people with OCD, the thought lingers and lingers. The anger and anxiety comes back over and over. The repeating grows and grows. The compulsion of numbers and sets grow and grow. It is a very frustrating situation. All of this from a comment from a friend. Nothing more.

Here's another example: Let's say you sit down to pay your bills. You open your healthcare bill. You notice that the due date is a few days before. The bill is past due. You get a thought of "Oh no!". The OCD kicks in. The thought gets stronger and stronger. You calm the thought down by thinking about the reality of it. The reality is that there is a grace period of thirty days for them to receive your payment before they cancel your policy. The payment will only be a few days late. All will be fine. The problem is that the OCD thought begins and keeps going for a few hours. So, the compulsion is to repeat "There is a grace period. I paid it within the grace period. I paid the bill.". This will continue just like the other examples I have given you. I will end up repeating a few sets in a few different places. This might go into a second day of repeating. This all because I opened and paid a bill after the actual due date but before the cancellation deadline. This could happen to anyone. The reason that is considered a normal thought is because it is real. You might pay a bill late. Your healthcare policy might be canceled if the company does not receive payment. The difference is that the OCD sends you into a thought which turns into an obsession. The obsession turns into the numbers and sets of repeating. This could last multiple days.

My last example of a normal or real obsession is a project at work. Let's say your boss gives you an important report to create. It is a Friday night. It is due for a meeting on Monday morning. You are the only one working on it. Your boss gives you little in the way of direction. Then your boss leaves early for the weekend. You have a basic understanding of what needs to be done. You work on it for a few hours. You are not one hundred percent positive that it is done correctly. It might not be what the boss actually wants. You did it with little direction and feel it is good enough. The thought that it is not done correctly lingers. You get an anxious thought that you screwed up the report. The OCD takes up the thought and it lingers and lingers. You finally leave the office. The compulsion is to repeat "It's fine. I will have time to fix it on Monday morning before the meeting. I'm sure that's what the boss wants. I am sure it's okay. They will not be mad. It will be fine." This continues just like the other thoughts. It ends up with a ton of anxiety and repeating. The thought does not go away. You end up doing the repeating. It might go into five sets of five in five places. Again, it will go into two days. This is all because your boss asks for a simple report. It happens in every office, in every building, in every city, in every country all over the world. For someone with OCD, it is two days of a lingering thought, repeating and anxiety. The reason this is a normal thought is due to the fact that everyone wants to impress their boss by doing a good job. You want to get the report done correctly the first time. You want to look good to your boss and the company. You don't want your boss to get mad or make you re-do the report over and over. The point is that it is something that everyone deals with. The difference with OCD is that it becomes a major two day issue.

To sum up normal or real thoughts and obsessions: They are focused on a response to a particular occurrence in everyday life. Because the parameters are narrower, I think of these as micro thoughts. They are perfectly normal life events. The difference is the O or Obsession portion of the OCD. It is the reason that a thought lingers. The OCD keeps the thought lingering. The lingering thought leads to the compulsions. The compulsions are designed to remove the lingering thoughts. The anxiety spikes on tiny little issues like a late bill or a poor joke at a dinner party. Once you get the thought, the anxiety kicks in, the depression kicks in from the anxiety. The compulsions begin to diffuse it all. The bottom line is that these real thoughts are usually something small and insignificant. Most people would not even think about it. The problem with having OCD is that these little micro thoughts blow up on you and will last minutes, hours, days or longer. Most people would not even have these thoughts or if they do, they might have them for a few seconds at most. Then they are over and done. Never to return. They think nothing of it. The thoughts that most people take for granted are horrible for people with OCD. Most people just do their errands on a warm Saturday afternoon. Someone like me does the errands, but they don't end there. There is tons and tons of OCD maintenance in order to do a simple, mundane, everyday routine errand. It can be pretty difficult.

And so we come to compulsions. It is the basic process of the OCD. It is what can make cognitive behavior therapy hard to do. It stems from doing the compulsions for years and knowing that it is easier to do the compulsion and move on than sit in anxiety for hours and wait until the obsession dissipates. It is what I will call force of habit caused by surrendering to the compulsions for years on end. The compulsions are simple cleanup procedures. You end up living extremely reactionary to the things that happen inside your body.

The way it works is that you get used to doing things a certain way. Think of something that you do in your life. Maybe you like to cook. You are right handed so you keep all of the utensils, bowls and ingredients on the right side of the stove. You add your ingredients in a specific order. You like to try new recipes. You always put the recipe in a certain place on the counter. The bottom line is that is just the way you like to cook. That is your system. That is what makes you feel comfortable. It is just the way you work. No matter what recipe you are trying or even if its an old recipe. The point is that you will do it this way.

Imagine that you are attempting a new recipe. You are nervous as you have never cooked this dish. You don't know if it will be good or not. You are not sure if you have chosen the right thing to make. This is the first time that you have ever used the specific spices that the recipe calls for. You are standing in your kitchen ready to begin. There is something odd. All of your utensils are on the left side of the stove. The pot is on a different burner. The recipe is folded on the right side of the stove. The spices are not out. All of your measuring tools are in the wrong place. Your entire kitchen is out of order. The point is that your usual way of cooking is different. Will you still be able to cook? Yes! Will the recipe still come out right? Yes! Will it taste good? Yes! You will just have to do it differently. You will need to look around for the stuff you need. You will need to change the way you do things. You will need to cook a different way. It might take some time to get used to. It might be frustrating. It might even be a better system than you had. But, the first time you cook in the new way, it will feel weird. You will not be comfortable. You will feel like something is out of whack. You will feel like you are cooking wrong. Like something is not correct. Something is wrong. Something doesn't feel comfortable cooking this way. It is not right. It is stressful and uncomfortable. It's just not the way you do things. You need to change the way you cook. You need to alter the way you function in your own kitchen. Bottom line: you will feel strange. You will feel like something is wrong or incomplete.

I used the cooking analogy for a reason. Not just to remind you that it might be time for you to start dinner. I did not even use it to get you to try a new recipe this weekend. I used it to show you that this is how people with OCD feel when they do not do or complete their compulsions.

The compulsions are big in the world of OCD. It is a major part of how we live. It is the true reason that the behavior therapy is so difficult. We just don't feel right when we do not do or finish the compulsions. The compulsions are what makes us feel that everything is alright. That everything is done and completed correctly. That everything is done and over. That all is right with the world. A person will feel that something is not quite right or off somehow if the compulsions are not done. This is especially true when the compulsions are not done perfectly and to the 'T'. Our body is just like your kitchen. If something is off, it will not feel right. Something will always feel off. The bottom line is that, with OCD, it is just the way we do things. Business as usual.

A person with OCD will feel weird if they do not do the compulsions. It will feel different. It will not feel right. This is the reason for the force of habit compulsions. You just feel better or right in doing them. You assign numbers to things and just do them. It is a simple number system. The numbers are always your specific "Right" numbers. They are always your "Right" sets as well. It is important to note that the obsession itself begins to fade. It is now just the plain and simple numbers compulsion. You do a specific thing a certain number of times. You just do it. You just move on.

There is one major issue with the force of habit compulsions. Remember, I mentioned that with the first two types of obsessions, there is a thought attached. The thought begins the process. You get a thought and then do some compulsions in order to relieve it. The force of habit compulsion flips the process around. It begins with the compulsion. If the compulsion is not completed correctly, then an obsessive thought is created. You must then continue to perform the compulsion in order to relieve the thought. Basically, there is no additional thought until you resist the OCD by not doing the compulsion. This is a third and very different type of obsession. With OCD, you get so used to doing the compulsions that it become natural, hence the term: "force of habit". You just automatically do it. This is why I am sure a lot of the people just do the compulsions. It is just easier. You end up feeling more comfortable doing them and so it become just a way of life. Do all the compulsions and that is your life. Having said that, when you do not do or complete the compulsions, then a new obsessive thought begins. The second you stop in the middle of a force of habit compulsion is when this third type of obsession

occurs. The thought comes after the compulsions have begun. If you resist or stop in the middle of a set of numbers, then you will get an obsession.

The only time that the force of habit compulsions get into larger numbers and sets is due to being in the middle of a bad OCD day. This is when you have an irrational or normal thought that is lingering. The force of habit compulsion tends to grow or increase when you are upset or having a bad day. A bad day could be filled with emotions, stress, anxiety, fighting larger irrational thoughts or normal thoughts and spending the entire day on completing compulsions. All of which make the force of habit compulsions get even worse.

Let's check out this example. If I say something to someone on this particular day, I may feel like I need to talk in numbers. There is no conscious irrational obsession. There is no conscious normal thought. I just feel like talking in numbers. I do not have any anxiety. There is no emotion. I just feel like talking in numbers. I want to make sure that you understand the distinction. This is not repeating. The repeating is where you need to say the exact same sentence or a specific word in a sentence a certain number of times. An example would be "I like cake.", "I like cake.", "I like cake.". See how it is the exact same sentence? It might also be "I like cake.", "Do you like cake?", "I feel like some cake.". The repeating word is "Cake". See how you can repeat a specific single word in a sentence? This is completely different. It is just talking in numbers. Plain and simple. I might be talking to someone and the numbers hit. Now I feel like I need to say three or five things. They can be the same subject matter or a completely different subject matter.

Here is an example of this type of force of habit using the same subject matter. Let's say the subject is a simple haircut. Most people would get a haircut and come home or go out with friends. They would say "I just got a haircut. What do you think?". If the reaction is positive, then they might add a "Thanks." That would be it. It would end right there and they would move on.

I would say "I got a haircut." The feeling to talk in numbers will show up. It will be light and have little to no anxiety. I am so used to the feeling. I am also so used to talking in numbers as I do it all the time. I will, through force of habit, just do it and get past it. So, I already said that "I got a haircut" which counts as one. I will add "Do you like it?" for number two. Then "It's not too short" for three. "They did a good job" for four. Then wait. Why wait? Because that is four and I will get a response. They say "Looks good". Now my answer is "Thank You" which is five. Do you see how that worked out to be five sentences on the same subject of haircuts.

Here is how the above example would work on completely different subject matters. I ask a friend "Do you like to cook?". This would trigger the slight feeling that I need to talk in numbers. It becomes force of habit as I usually do the compulsion. I asked "Do you like to cook?" which counts as one. I ask "Do you like to travel?" which is two. "I would love to take a class to learn more about wine" which is three. I say "How do you like your new apartment?" which is four. Finally, I add "How's work?" which is five. Please note that my friend answered all of the questions in between. For the purpose of this discussion, I just included my questions. Do you see how I was able to talk in a set of five about five different subjects?

Here is another example of a force of habit compulsion where there is no thought involved. Let's say I am shaving. Men do it every day all over the world. I have a traditional force of habit compulsion that always occurs. I shave the right side of my face and then the left. I always feel like I need to shave the left side one extra time. Why the left? Who knows. Sometimes I might feel that I did not shave the left side perfectly or that I did not shave my face evenly. It is just what happens. I usually just do the compulsion and shave the left side a little more. This entails running the electric razor down the left side of my face three extra times. If I don't do the compulsion, I just feel odd or that something is not done right. There is nothing else that happens. Just a weird incomplete feeling. If I notice a few extra hairs on the right side, I will just shave them. Then, in true OCD fashion, I will go back to the left and do the set of three. It happens each and every shave. So, I just do the compulsion and move on with my day.

Here is an example of a force of habit compulsion where an obsession might occur. Let's say I am writing a book on my computer. Gee, I wonder where that idea came from. I write a few pages. It is time for a break. I save my file. I just save it three or five times. Not a big deal. But, if I stop in the middle of the set, I will then get a small and quick obsession with no anxiety. The thought would be that since I did not complete the set or do it the correct number of times, I will lose everything that I just wrote. The reality is that if I save it once, it is saved. It will be saved whether you save it one time or three hundred. Still, the obsession can occur if the number compulsion is not completed.

Here is another example of force of habit when a thought is attached. I usually go out my front door and check it a quick set of five. This is done by trying to turn the door handle to make sure that it does not turn and open the door. I do it every time and quickly. Let's say that I go out, close the door and only check the door handle four or six times. I will start to walk away. An obsession will bloom. It will be a very quick and small thought. It will not have anxiety attached. It is just due to the fact that I did not do the force of habit compulsion correctly. If I do not go back and do another set of five on the front door, I will feel uncomfortable. I might have thoughts that I will get robbed or someone will open my door and steal something from my house. The thought will not be too bad. It might be a little worse if I am having a bad day.

To sum up the force of habit obsessions: They are different than any other type of OCD. They do not begin with an obsession or anxiety. The obsessions are not the driving force behind the compulsions. The thought might come after the compulsions have begun. The anxiety, if it occurs, will be light. The thoughts and anxiety will only occur if you do not do the compulsions. They will also occur if you stop in the middle of a set of compulsions.

They differ from the other types of obsessions because they are just based on the numbers and sets of numbers. It is the pure compulsion. They are usually not caused by any kind of emotions such as anger, sadness or fear. They are just how you do things. They will always contain your "Right" numbers and sets. It is just a matter of doing them and nothing more. They are basically just the way you live. Most people leave their house and just slam the door behind them. I check my door a quick set of five. Most people just say something once. I say it three or five times. Most men just shave their face once. I shave the left a few extra times. Nothing major. It is just the way things are done in the world of OCD.

You might have different numbers for each thing you do. You might have the same numbers for everything all across the board. No matter how you do it. You will just do it and move on. The force of habit obsessions end very quickly. You get very used to having them. You know they will occur if you are about to lock as door or check a window or stove. It is just your system. There is no thought. There is no major feeling. There is usually no anxiety. It is just the numbers and sets of numbers you live with. You can live in a place for fifty years and you will check the front door the same number of times every time you shut the door.

As for me, I do not get flustered or upset. I just do these things whether I am having a good day or a bad day. I know that when I do a specific thing that there will always be numbers attached. I know that I will just do these things no matter how often they occur. There are specific tasks which will always have numbers. There are specific items that also have numbers. My numbers are three and five. That is why I will just do everything three or five times…Period. There might not be a thought. There might not be a feeling. There is just the numbers and sets of numbers. You don't need a real thought or an irrational obsession. You just feel better living in your numbers. It makes you feel a lot better and relaxed knowing that you did things the "Right" number of times. They are just the number of times you do any given task. Even if there is no thought, anxiety or obsession attached, you will do things this way. You will feel uncomfortable if you do not do things in numbers. You will feel like something is off or not quite completed correctly. The force of habit obsession will only show up if this premise is ignored.

Imagine that you are in your house. One night you decide to go to sleep without locking your front door. How will you feel? My guess is a little off, like you did not complete something. Maybe like you did not do something correctly. I am sure that the same feeling would occur if you parked your car at a crowded shopping mall and walked away without locking it. It would be unsettling at the least. Something was not done the usual way. The obsession that arrives after force of habit compulsions are not done, is just a little feeling that something is off or incomplete if something is done without the correct numbers or sets of numbers.

With OCD, you become sick of the "Off" feeling so you make sure to do it the right number of times. You know you will get the incomplete feeling without doing the compulsions. Doing the numbers and sets is the only way to stay away from these feelings. You know it will happen. You do not want to have to deal with it or sit in it. The reality is that the "Off" feeling will get stronger and stronger. It might last longer and longer. Then the "Off" feeling will linger just like the other obsessions. Why would you want to deal with that if you can check a door five times and be free? So, you just do it. It's easier. You get used to it. You get good at it so that it becomes easier and easier. You do the numbers quick and extremely fast. You learn that it takes less time to do it than dealing with a thought that might linger. So, it becomes easier to just do the force of habit compulsion than not doing it. Why sit with an "Off" feeling if you can fix it? Especially because the number will only take a few seconds or minutes to complete. Anyone who has this type of obsession knows that doing the compulsion and getting past it is the only way to move their day forward. It is much faster to just complete the compulsion and move your life on. It is just how someone with OCD does things. This is why they are a force of habit.

Here are my final thoughts about obsessions and the compulsions they partner with: I have outlined three different types of obsessions. I wanted to show that there are different types of obsessions. Most of the medical professionals that I have spoken to list all of these thoughts as obsessions. It is one blanket term. Maybe that is how they understand Obsessive Compulsive Disorder. They only focus on the general categories. I wanted to show that a person can have more than one type of obsession. Each type of obsession has a different type of feeling. Each type has a different reason for doing a compulsion. All of these types are the same in the fact that they linger. They may cause or be caused by anxiety. They all become worse with anxiety. They all fluctuate if you are having a bad day. They all get worse with emotions. They all might last for hours or even days.

The irrational thought is a thought that is not really possible. It is usually obvious that is it irrational and impossible. Most of them are scary in nature and cause fear in the person with OCD.

The normal or real thought is a thought that is real. It

is also possible. It is based on a usual everyday life event. The person with OCD might feel an emotion such as anger, sadness or fear. A normal or real obsession is a thought that just lingers. Now, imagine if each and every one of the basic daily thoughts lingered for hours or days. Each thought leads to repeating compulsions that have to be done in sets and numbers. The thoughts might even lead to multi day lingering and repeating. The person with OCD will suffer the same as if it was an irrational thought.

The force of habit thought is compulsion based. There is usually no thought or obsession. There is no anxiety. There might be a thought or obsession if the compulsion is not done correctly. The thought or obsession is not the driving force of these types of compulsions. They are led by the compulsions themselves. The thoughts / obsessions only occur if the compulsions are not done correctly. These are not the usual pattern or else it would be called Compulsion Obsession Disorder. Someone with OCD has their certain numbers that they are comfortable with. They assign these numbers to everyday tasks.

Imagine everything you do in one day and add a number to it. You lock your front door, make sure you have your car keys or credit card, turn off the oven, check your phone, grab your wallet, satisfy yourself that you got everything on your list for the market, review the ingredients needed for a new recipe, pay bills, prepare reports at work, workout at the gym, prepare for a vacation, complete your errands, etc. Now, imagine that you have to do each and every one of these things a certain number of times. The certain numbers might turn into multiple sets. It is just the way that you do things with OCD. You end up just doing all of the force of habit compulsions. It makes for a very busy day.

The disorder is called Obsessive Compulsive Disorder for a reason. The Obsessions are half of the title for a reason. Obsessions are a huge part of living with this disorder. Someone with OCD spends half of their time in a day dealing with obsessions.

The same person with OCD spends the other half of their day dealing with Compulsions or attempts at Cognitive Behavior Therapy which never worked for me. (see Chapter 12) The obsessions might be irrational, real or a force of habit. They cause anxiety. They can happen hourly or daily. They are difficult to deal with whether they are large or small. Whether they last long or go away immediately. They can make you mad, scared or angry. They can cause a ton of depression just having to deal with them. Day in and day out.

CHAPTER 4: ANXIETY!

"Lots of Knots!"

Anxiety is a huge part of OCD. It is the physical reaction of most intrusive obsessions. Anxiety can stop you from doing something. It will also drive you to doing something even more, such as a compulsion. The anxiety can dictate how your entire day goes. Anxiety fuels the fire of OCD.

The basic way that anxiety fits into the OCD is the ability that it has to strengthen the obsessive thoughts. The overall rule is that the higher the level of anxiety that is caused by an irrational thought, the higher the chance is that it will increase your fear that the thought or feeling is real. The anxiety dictates the level of the OCD and your reaction to it. If the anxiety is high, the compulsions are usually larger and more detailed. The thoughts will be stronger and last longer. The compulsions will last longer. The entire system will have a lot more strength. If the anxiety is low, the compulsions are usually quick and easy. The thoughts are much weaker and do not last as long. Either way, if you have OCD, you will need to get used to anxiety.

Anxiety will ruin your day. It will at the least, make you feel very uncomfortable. It will feel like a knot tightly wound in your stomach. It will seem like you are shaking or vibrating at a high level. You will be very upset and off kilter. You will feel unnerved. You will instantly know something is very wrong. We all have a form of this agitation.

Having anxiety that is fueled by a thought or feeling hurts. You feel helpless and very depressed that you have to go through this kind of stress. It is painful emotionally. You feel fear and depression when the obsessive thought takes hold of you. In an instant, the obsessive thought gets worse and so do the compulsions.

I know many people may think that most people with OCD have some form of social anxiety. This is not at all true. There is no fear of socializing in itself. The lack of being social is due to the obsessions that trigger when we are in our daily lives. It is a different type of fear. It is a fear that the OCD will start up. Because then, the priority is to deal with it and try to hide the compulsions that we are doing. This is what makes socializing very difficult.

The anxiety will appear after an obsession in many different ways. It might hit instantly or gradually build up. It might shoot in like a lightning bolt at a high level. It might start out very low and gradually increase. You can just be sitting there and get a thought and bingo; a belt of anxiety.It will always be painful and horrible and might come with a lingering buzz.

The longer the thought stays around, the longer the anxiety will. It will also get stronger and stronger if the thought persists. The anxiety will also make the compulsions stronger and last longer as well. It will sort of glue the obsession and the compulsion together. They are tied together until you can find a way to extricate yourself.

The way that the obsession, anxiety and compulsions work together is a very intricate balance. You will get an obsessive thought and then the anxiety will hit. The anxiety will convince you that the thought is true or real. The anxiety will control the amount of the compulsions that must be done as well as the duration. You will get a small feeling prior to the anxiety that something is wrong. The obsessive thought will use that to get stronger. Once it is stronger, you will get more anxiety. You will need to do more compulsions. The more anxiety you get, the stronger the thought becomes and the longer
it lingers. The longer it lingers, the stronger the thought gets.

The compulsions increase at the same pace. Does that even make sense? It is a very harmful system.

Anxiety will make you extremely uncomfortable and will dictate the believability of your thought. The amount of believability the thought has will dictate your entire day and the compulsions that you do. If you really believe the thought is real, you are more likely to get locked into an entire day of compulsions. You will really want to complete them no matter how long they are. The higher the anxiety becomes, the more that the behavior therapy (CBT) does not work.

Having anxiety is really painful. You have to try to function with a stomach full of butterflies. It is very difficult as you cannot relax. You will need to act as if you are fine when you are really not. You might get hit with anxiety when you are at a dinner party, with friends, family, coworkers, or even trying to sleep. It is very difficult to focus on anything or anyone when you are in a dire stage of anxiety. You have to maintain your composure as well as continue conversations, eat healthy, do your errands and maintain personal care. It is like constantly swimming upstream.

If you are in a social situation or at your job when the anxiety hits, it is even worse. You have to act like nothing is wrong. People are with you that are mostly at ease while you have tremendous anxiety. You have to try and seem normal even with a deadly bouquet of anxiety. Not fun at all.

Let me try to explain it to you with some examples. For these examples, I will use the traditional one to ten scale. One meaning the anxiety is very low. Ten meaning the anxiety is awful and very high.

My first example is with a typical thought. I drive home. I park my car, get out and lock it. I then begin to walk away. All of a sudden I get a thought. The thought is that I did not lock the car at all. I get an anxiety level at about two. I then feel that I need to do a compulsion of beeping the car alarm another two times. So

I do it. The anxiety is low and stays low. Maybe it is the fact that I am used to that particular thought as I get it a lot.

My next example is with a stronger thought. I was river rafting with a few friends. I was in a boat with five people. It was myself, a friend and his kids. We were all enjoying the ride. Suddenly we went down a particular bumpy rapid. We all were banged around a little. I had bumped into my friend's son. He was fine. I immediately had an obsession that I had hurt him very badly. I got hit with an anxiety level of ten. It was pretty strong. I apologized for bumping him. He said that it was no problem. He was not hurt at all. Still, the obsession persisted. It got worse and worse. I had a compulsion to keep checking on him by just looking and seeing if he was actually okay. The thought was pretty bad. There I was with a ton of strong anxiety. The odd part is that the anxiety was due to the obsession and not the huge rapids we were all flying down. Most people would have been focused on the rapids. I was focused on my friend's son. Mind you, I already knew that he was fine. This shows you how persistent the OCD is. The priority should have been the task at hand like, I don't know, shooting down class four rapids? It makes no sense whatsoever! The anxiety and the obsession lasted all day. I did the compulsions and the anxiety lowered. It robbed me of the excitement and the enjoyment of the day.

My next example is a time when I went shopping. I was walking down one of the aisles in the grocery store. I reached out to buy a bottle of olive oil. I accidently touched the next bottle over that was on the shelf. I immediately thought that I pushed the bottle close enough to the edge and it would fall and smash on the floor. This would either hurt someone by falling or cause the store a loss when the bottle breaks. The anxiety was very low at about a one. It lasted for a few aisles and then subsided. I knew that if I reacted to it, the OCD would take advantage and get worse and worse. The compulsion was to repeatedly check the aisle. I needed to see that the bottle of olive oil would not fall. I continued doing my shopping. As I began finding the rest of my groceries, the thought of the olive oil bottle got stronger and stronger. The anxiety went from a one to a three and then to an eight. I just wanted it to end so I went back to the aisle and checked the olive oil. As you can guess, it was fine and nothing was going to fall. I did the compulsions and the anxiety went away.

Here is another example: I was sitting on my couch, simply watching TV. I started to think of calling a friend. It was very late at night. I realized that I forgot my cell phone in my car. I immediately got a thought that it would get stolen. This is an example of a lightning bolt of anxiety. I immediately was hit with anxiety at a level of ten. It skyrocketed immediately and then subsided to about an eight. I went out to my car and retrieved my cell phone. Then I walked back inside. The second I got my phone, the anxiety dropped. Here is a typical example of how someone with OCD is prone to anxiety. I got high anxiety with an obsession. There was no formal compulsion to do. I just needed to find my cell phone in my car and that was it. The anxiety dropped instantly. Basically, I got tremendous anxiety for absolutely nothing.

I was talking to a friend of mine. We were discussing restaurants. I told him that a restaurant was good when it was sort of so so. I immediately got high anxiety. It was about an eight. The obsession was that I committed a major lie. I felt as if I lied to my close friend and the obsession hit. The anxiety was strong. I felt as if I needed to correct my major lie. The compulsion was to repeatedly tell him that the restaurant was just plain so so or average. I did the repeating compulsion by rewording my sentences. With each sentence or repeating, the anxiety got lower and lower. I went from an eight to a five and then a two. I did the compulsion and the anxiety went away and so did the obsession.

My next example is of a medium dose of anxiety. I washed my hands. I went to dry my hands. I counted that I dried my hands four times. Four is not a good number for me. I immediately felt a medium level of anxiety. The anxiety was at around a five. The compulsion was to dry my hands another time to make it five times total. I did the compulsion and the anxiety lowered and lowered until it was gone.

I was watching TV one night. I saw that there were two different shows on that I liked. I switched between them a few times. I ended up counting that I had switched between each show a total of three times. I got anxiety. It was a low amount at around a two. The compulsion was that I needed to make it a five. I needed to switch between both shows and change channels a total of five times. I did the compulsions and the anxiety went away.

My final example will include multi levels of anxiety. I was talking to someone about dinner and we planned to meet. My friend called me and told me that he needed to cancel. I said that it was fine and we went our separate ways. I then got a thought that we had never canceled and got a visual of my friend sitting in the restaurant and waiting for me. I immediately got anxiety. The anxiety was at around a five. I said to myself that we canceled dinner. I repeated it one time. A few seconds minutes later, I was outside on my patio. I had the obsession again. I started to wonder if we actually did cancel dinner. I got anxiety at around a six. I felt to repeat once more that we had canceled our dinner. The numbers automatically started up and now I needed to repeat in three or five places. If you remember, I had already repeated in the house and then on my patio so that was two places. I started to do the compulsions and went into my house to repeat that we had canceled dinner inside the house to make it a set of three. The anxiety lowered for a second. Then it skyrocketed and I needed to repeat in and out of the house five times. It can be exhausting.

The way that the anxiety works is that it will usually raise and lower depending on the level of fear created by your obsession. Do you believe that the thought is actually real and possible? The more that you believe it, the stronger the anxiety will be. The less you fear or believe it, the less the anxiety will be. As an example of this, think of your car. If you feared that it would be stolen; hey, cars can be stolen. If you had a thought that the car was going to be stolen by aliens from another planet, it is not as believable so the anxiety would be lower. You see how this works?

Another thing to keep in mind is that the anxiety within a thought will raise and lower as the cycle evolves. It will do this depending on how you do the compulsions. As you do the compulsions, the anxiety will lower. Then, it will return. It will return when you feel that you need to do more compulsions. The higher number of compulsions will bring a higher amount of anxiety. The opposite is also true. The lower the amount of compulsions will usually have lower anxiety.

The horrible part of anxiety is that it can control you. It can make you stop in your tracks. It is like you are frozen in time. You cannot eat, laugh, relax or do anything. You cannot enjoy a movie, dinner, dessert or even playing with a pet. You cannot sleep or eat. It is extremely sad.

The anxiety is a major piece of OCD. It is very painful to have to sit and act like everything is fine when you are consumed by a huge amount of anxiety. It can be very difficult. This is especially true when you are trying to complete something or stay involved in something like a dinner party or other social engagement. Connections to other people are very important to all of us.

I have woken up with pure anxiety and had to try to sleep with total anxiety. This is not an easy task whatsoever. People with OCD are prone to having anxiety. We tend to get anxiety over things that most people do not even give a second thought to.

The anxiety can sneak up on you in a second; or gradually grow. Just remember, the anxiety level depends on how much you believe the thought. Let's say that I come into my house. I come in through the front door and then lock the door behind me. I jiggle the handle three times by force of habit to make sure that it is locked. I walk away from the door. I then get an obsession. The obsession is that my life will change or be changed in some way. The obsessions that wreak havoc on me always have a compulsion attached. In this case, the compulsion was that I needed to check the door five sets of five or my life would be different. Yeah, like I am a completely different person if I don't check the front door a certain amount of time. Whatever! Anyway, I get a low level of anxiety. It is about a two. I then tell myself to do the behavior therapy (CBT) and ignore the thought. Then, the anxiety instantly gets higher and raises to about a four or five. I know that the thought is just an obsession and is completely fake. I tell myself that I am doing the behavior therapy. I then start to feel that my life will actually be different. Then, the anxiety goes up to about a ten. It is awful. If you remember what I said, the level of anxiety is controlled and depends on how much you actually believe the thought. So, I know am starting to believe the thought. This causes the anxiety to flare up even more. I am now very uncomfortable. I know the reality is that the thought is completely untrue. I still start to believe it and that my life will actually be different if I do not do the compulsions which skyrockets the anxiety even more. Then, I just break down and say "Screw It!" and do the stupid compulsions. As I begin to do the compulsions, the anxiety starts to lower. Then, I take another stand and say that I am not doing it. Then the anxiety gets worse. It raises a little. I then begin doing the compulsions again and the anxiety lowers again. I then take a stand and threaten to do the behavior therapy and the anxiety gets worse. I finally have had it. I completely give in and do all of the compulsions and the thought and anxiety completely disappear. Do you see how the second you believe the thought, the anxiety gets worse? That is the way that it works. The more that you believe the thought, the stronger the anxiety will be. The less you believe the thought, the less the anxiety will be. The anxiety will start with the thought and then lower as you do the compulsions. The anxiety will come back strong if you decide to stop doing the compulsions.

In conclusion, people with OCD live in anxiety. There are some days that we have anxiety all day and some days not at all. We all live with it. It can be hard to relax at times and just enjoy our daily lives. It is a silent thing that we all suffer with. It makes life very hard. No matter what, if you have OCD, you will need to get used to living with anxiety. It can be hard at times and easy during other times. Either way, it sucks!

CHAPTER 5: DOUBT!

*"I Don't Think I Ever Needed To Write
This Chapter...Or Did I?"*

Doubt is a part of life. Everyone has it at one point or another. Hopefully, doubt can be solved by a simple action. We have all uttered the phrases: "Did I lock the car?", "Did I turn the stove off?", "Did I turn the coffee pot off?", "Did I say something wrong?", Did I make the wrong decision?". These issues are all very commonplace. This kind of doubt usually happens when we are rushing to complete several tasks at once. Each of these things come with an easy to use remedy. Just double back on the darn thing! Go back in the house and re-check to make sure the stove is off and the coffee pot is off. Walk back to the front door and check to make sure it is actually locked. Walk back to the car, press the remote, listen for the beep and voila, the car is locked. It is a very simple process. It happens to people of any age all over the world. When it does happen, it does not last long at all. It is not difficult to deal with. It does not stop your day or ruin your life. It is not uncomfortable or painful. It is just what it is...a minor fact of life.

It is a completely different story for people with OCD. For many people with OCD, doubt is a major factor in life and is a type of obsession. The thought descends and it can be created by any routine event in your day. It can also affect multiple days. The level of doubt can change. The level is usually dictated by the outcome of the event that transpired. Basically, it depends on the situation.

Doubt is another large part of OCD. It is intertwined in

the entire system. There is a lot of doubt that can occur in one day and fuel the symptoms. The doubt within the OCD comes in the form of a thought. The thought is that you did not do or complete something. This doubtful thought becomes the bridge to the compulsions, replacing the anxiety, sort of a middle "Feeling" that hits within seconds of doing something. Like the rest of the OCD thoughts, both rational and irrational, the doubtful thought will linger. It will linger and linger until the compulsion shows up. The little thought of doubt happens in a matter of milliseconds. The second it happens; you start to feel the feeling that you need to perform some sort of compulsion.

It is not always doubt that fuels the compulsions, but it does happen a lot. The thought or feeling of doubt is very uncomfortable. Each and every form of doubt leads you to do a different type of compulsion. These compulsions are your usual ones. The doubt is triggered immediately after an event. Then, if the compulsion is not performed correctly, the doubtful thought will linger. It will linger until you start to feel like doing the compulsion. Then, if you are like me, you will hate the feeling and you will begin to perform the compulsion. Once you begin the compulsion process, the doubt will return in between each compulsion in order to get you to do another set. It will continue. Once you completed one set, then you are in the numbers and sets. Then the OCD will take it from there and keep going. The bottom line is that you will then be in the traditional compulsions. The feelings of the number, sets and overall anxiety where you need to complete the compulsion perfectly will begin. It will keep going and going. You will be trapped. You will remain in this position until the compulsions are completed perfectly. The entire process starts with the doubt. The second the doubt hits, the process has begun. The second you do something and the doubt hits, you might be doing compulsions for days. It all starts with a dumb little act that you perform and instantly, a few days of your life will be very anxiety ridden and busily filled with compulsions and other repetitions.

The equation is: Little Act + Doubt = Compulsions! The doubt can happen in many different ways. The compulsion needed will depend solely on the level of doubt. Basically, what the doubt is, will dictate the exact compulsion needed. Remember that the level of the doubt depends on the perceived outcome of the event involved. The doubt can manifest as one of two things. The causal event can be something verbally or physically that you did. It can also be something that you did not do. Either way, it is difficult to have to deal with. Once you get to the compulsions, anxiety will kick in. The amount of anxiety depends on the number of compulsions that you determine need to be completed. It can be large or small. The larger the consequence, the more the compulsions needed will multiply, and the longer it all will last. The small and insignificant outcome will equal a much smaller and easier compulsion. This compulsion will be much weaker. It will also not linger or last as long. The compulsions are usually very small and quick to accomplish. No big deal. Now, let's look at some examples.

The first thing that I should clarify is that there are three major different types of doubt related obsessions. The first is a doubt with a "Real" or "Possible" consequence. The second is a doubt with a "Believable" or "Perceived" consequence. The third is a doubt with a "Traditional" or "Force Of Habit" consequence. Either way, the results of all three are the same. Definitely not fun! No matter which one you get, you will have some compulsions to complete. Now that I probably confused the living hell out of you, I will explain each. Don't worry. It will make sense at some point.

There is the "Real or Possible" doubt. I define the doubt with a "Real" or "Possible" outcome as something that can actually happen from an action you performed or have not performed. This "Real" consequence is when something is actually important or actually matters. The event can cause you to worry about something real. The reality is that, if you feel as if you did not lock the front door, this doubtful thought will make you worry that your house might get robbed. If you do not lock your car door, the car might get stolen. These are more realistic as far as thoughts go.

The first example of the "Real or Possible" doubt is with locking things. These can be home doors, office doors, a friend's house doors, a family member's house door, windows, cabinets, a safe and, of course, car doors. The reason that these are considered "Real or Possible" is because the consequences are real. It is a realistic fear or worry. Everybody worries about these things. Whether you have OCD or not, you will worry about these things. Let's face it, if you don't lock your car door, the car can actually get stolen. In the case of locking your car door, the doubt will show up. Let's say I park my car, get out of the car, close the door and beep my alarm. Now notice a few things: I physically saw myself close the car door, heard it slam, heard a car horn honk when I hit the alarm, and heard the doors lock. Having OCD, the second I turn my head away and begin to walk away, the doubt sets in. I will immediately wonder and be unsure that I locked the door at all. I just don't know. It happens that fast. The second I start to walk away from the car, I will doubt my actions. As I walked further away, the doubt will get stronger. The anxiety will get stronger. The visuals will get stronger. I will have a visual of coming back to an empty parking space. I will feel that something is not complete. I will be anxious that I did not lock my car. This will lead to a checking compulsion. I will feel the need to re check the car. I will beep the car alarm one more time. This will start the numbers. I will beep the car alarm three or five times. Then I will begin to walk away. I will then turn around one more time. The second I turn around that extra time, the numbers will increase. I will now have to turn around and check the car three or five more times. The reality is that without OCD, a person would just check one more time and be done. Then go about their day. With OCD you get the fun of all thoughts, visuals and compulsions. This example was with the car. The exact same process will happen if I locked anything   at all. It can be a car, a boat, a house, windows, doors, etc. Seems like fun right?

The next example is with household appliances. We all use them. We all turn them off. With OCD it is not that easy; whether you are turning off a stove, an oven, a coffee pot, a toaster oven, a panini press or a crockpot. Either way, the doubt will occur. Let me explain it to you. Let's say I am cooking pasta. When the pasta is done I turn off the stove. The second I turn my head or leave the room, the doubt will come in. I will immediately get anxiety and the feeling that something is not complete. I will get a visual that the stove is on. The visual might have fire coming out of the burners or catching a roll of paper towels on fire. Either way, I'm in for the long haul. I will come check the stove one more time. This will ignite the numbers. I will now have to check it three or five times. Since I came back into the kitchen, that made it a set of two. This will mean that I will need to come back into the kitchen to check the stove three or five times. So now, I will need to walk into the kitchen and walk back out three or five times. While I'm in the kitchen I will need to check the stove three to five times. This is what's known as sets of compulsions. As you can see, this would be a realistic fear. If you do not turn off your appliances, you can cause a fire. This is what the OCD feeds on. It is basically a real fear that leads to a series of compulsions that can last anywhere from an hour to a day or two days.

The final example for this is shopping. For this example, let's use my credit card. We could be at a restaurant, store, mall, movie theater, car wash, food hall, getting our hair cut, grocery store, tailor, etc. Basically anywhere we will use a credit card. You will pay for your stuff. You will take your credit card back or pull it out of a machine. You will put it wherever you keep it. With OCD, it works differently. I will pay for whatever I have. Put the card away. Then the obsession will begin. I will get the doubt mixed with anxiety. I will worry whether I have my credit card. Did I get the right card back? Did I get the card back at all? Did I drop the card on the floor? There will be a visual of my card sitting on the floor of the store.

The reason this is a real fear is because credit cards do get stolen. That is a real thing. It can actually happen. People do steal other people's credit cards. If someone found your credit card, they could buy stuff and put charges on your balance. This will cause you to have to call the credit card company and prove that you did not buy those things. It will be a major hassle and cause you anxiety. This is a real fear that everyone has. It is perfectly normal. We all have it. With OCD, this will cause you to do the compulsion. The compulsion for me will be to reach into my wallet and check to make sure I have my credit card three or five times. I will only do it once or the sets will kick in while I am in public. I will take my credit card out of my wallet one time and look at it by moving my eyes back-and-forth. I will make sure to visually look at the card three or five times. That's it. Still having fun?

There is the "Believable" doubt. I define the doubt with no real consequence as a "Believable" outcome. This is a consequence that is not an actual possibility or a reality. There is no real thing to fear or worry about. It is basically something that is only important to the individual with OCD. This might include the fact that you did not tell somebody something that the doubtful feeling makes you think is very important. The truth is that it is not important at all.

Let's say that someone did something nice for you. Let's make it a birthday gift. So, it is your birthday and you are having dinner with your friends and family. Then, after dinner, the entire crowd moves to another room. You walk in and there are cards and gifts on the coffee table. You, your friends and family, all get comfortable in the room. Someone hands you a gift and a card. You open it and thank them. Or did you? You said "Thank You". You know that you did. You heard yourself say it, "Thank You". The person reacted to it and said "You are welcome". With OCD, you will say "Thank You" and immediately not know that you said it. You will have a blank feeling. You will feel like you just sat there, took the gift, opened it and said nothing. The logic that you know that you did the right thing means nothing. You will still feel as if you were rude or did not thank them for their generous gift. You feel like you were mean to them. As you sit with the doubt, the anxiety will build. Then the obsessions will begin. The obsessions or thoughts will be something like you not thanking them for the gift or they did not hear you. You did not say it loud enough. They were talking so they did not hear you properly. This will include every variation of not thanking them. The longer that you sit in it, the worse the obsessions get. You will feel as if you were ungrateful. This is after you were so sure that you heard yourself say it. You will feel that the person or people are mad at you or that they will mention to someone else that you did not thank them and were very rude. Do you see why I consider this a "Believable" doubt? It is believable but has no real consequences. The reality is that the worst case scenario is that you did not thank someone one year for a gift when in a crowd. The person will completely understand. They will not even be thinking of it after the exchange. The reality is that it was nothing. You know that you really did thank them. You know that you did. You even saw them look at you and say "You are welcome". But still, the OCD will do its thing. The OCD will tell you that you did not thank them for the gift. Then, to remedy it, you need to thank them again. This will assure you or reassure you that you did in fact thank them. To do this, you thank them again. Then the numbers kick in and you keep saying thank you. For me, it will be three or five times. You will need to hide the repeating by saying it in different ways. Directly, at the end of a sentence and at the beginning of a sentence. The easiest way to get the repeating done and without people knowing is to say "thank you" right after you get the gift. Add a "I really love it thank you". Then, at the end of the night as you are walking out, one last repetition of "Again, thank you for the gift" will do it. This will complete the set of three. You finally thanked them three times. Great, Huh?

Here's another example. Let's say that you are at a friend's house. You just finished dinner. They cooked so you offer to clean up. While doing the dishes, you break a dish. Hey, it happens. Everyone knows it was an accident. You immediately apologize. The second you do, the OCD kicks in. you actually do not know that you apologized. This is why I call it a "Believable" doubt. The doubt is that you feel like you were rude or mean and did not say you were sorry for breaking a dish of theirs. You feel as if you were uncaring and that you smashed something. This is not true at all. You did apologize. You heard yourself apologize. You also heard and saw them accept it and tell you that it was okay. With OCD, you will still feel as if you did not say anything. This will increase the doubt, the anxiety and the uneasy feeling that something is unfinished. The only way to "know" that you apologized correctly is to get into the repeating in numbers. Basically, you will need to do the repeating compulsion. It can be done the same way as the birthday thank you. Twice in a row with a sentence in between. Then again as you are leaving for the night. You can say "Again, I'm sorry for breaking the dish". That's it. That is how it works.

The next example will be with a normal conversation. Let's say that you are with a friend. You are taking a trip the next day. They tell you that you will need to meet them by 6 AM in order to begin the long drive. This will help to get out of the city before the traffic gets bad. You will then say "OK". The doubt will kick right in. The doubt will make you wonder if you heard right. You will get the anxiety and the obsession. Was it 6 AM? Am I sure? Was I wrong? Did I hear wrong? Am I sure that it is 6 AM? Was it 8 AM or 9 AM? You will have two visuals. One will be your friend is mad that you are late. The other will be that they are mad because you are way too early. The way to correct it is to, as I say with OCD, triple check. This is where you would repeat on them a few times that you will see them at 6 AM. You will know that they will just correct you if it is the incorrect time. Once the repeating is done, the doubt will disappear.

The final example of a "Believable" doubt will be when you tell someone something. I will use an example of a work incident that happened to me. One Friday, my boss was leaving early. He stopped by my cubicle to let me know that he wanted our staff meeting to be at 11 AM on Monday. He then left. I now have the doubt of whether I heard him correctly or not. Did I hear the time right? Did I hear it incorrectly? The anxiety and the thought hit and began to linger. So, a few hours go by and I am in the kitchen getting some coffee. I am in the kitchen with a few co-workers. One co-worker asks another when the Monday staff meeting is. I quickly jump in and tell them that the boss told me that it was at 11 AM. They all agree that they will be there. They leave. There I am, standing in the kitchen filled with doubt. Did I hear the boss correctly? Did I tell the staff the correct time? I get the thought and the anxiety. The visuals are that the boss and entire staff will be angry with me if I screwed it up. The staff will show up early and have to wait. The boss will get there early and be pissed that he has to wait. He will be upset with the staff and they will be upset with me. The only way to solve this, as you don't want to repeat on everyone at work, is to just repeat on one person and the OCD will accept that. Then this incident is complete. Nice, Huh?

There is the "Traditional" doubt. This type of doubt is an automatic and traditional feeling from the OCD. It is sort of a force of habit obsession. This traditional type of doubt is the feeling that the OCD sufferer will get a lot. It can be intertwined in every type of obsession and / or compulsion. This OCD doubt only exists to continue the OCD process. It is the middle piece between the thought or feeling and the compulsions. It is the "Traditional" type of doubt that is basically compulsion based. It is the basic feeling you get when any compulsion starts up. It is what triggers the force of habit to complete each compulsion.

The doubt in combination with the force of habit compulsions is a difficult symptom to deal with. The first example I will use is simply conversational talking. When I am in a conversation, I will tell the other person something and instantly feel as if I did not say anything. This leads to usually unimportant repeating.

The next example will be with the numbers. The second I do a set of numbers, I have the doubt that I did them correctly, did them the right number of times, did them the wrong number of times or even did the compulsion at all. This will lead to doing the numbers in more and more sets.

The final example is with the saving a file on my computer. If it is an important file and I put a lot of effort into what I did, it is important to save it. I will obviously save it and immediately feel as if I did not save the file. This will lead to me saving the file three or five times. Basically, more number compulsions. After every set that you do, you will get the same doubt, thought and feelings. This will lead you into bigger and longer lasting sets of compulsions. It is a major portion of the OCD.

It is very difficult to live with doubt. I know most people use the term "Doubt" a lot. They say things like "Doubtful", "I Doubt That", I Doubt It", etc. When someone without OCD says that they doubt they did something, it usually either ends there or they double check something. Then they can simply move on with their day. With OCD, the world is filled with doubt. Your day is filled with doubt. The doubt is whether or not you said something, spoke, thanked someone, apologized to someone, did something correctly, did something incorrectly, locked something, touched something, repeated something, or all of the above.

My conclusion on the doubt is that it is the basic fuel or gasoline for the compulsions. It happens before the compulsions, during the compulsions and after the compulsions. It is not easy to live with. With OCD, the doubt can ruin your entire day. I doubt this chapter was important...see what I did there... hey, I thought that it was funny!

CHAPTER 6: THE NUMBERS!

"It's As Easy As 1, 2, 3!"

I have discussed many different aspects of the Obsessive Compulsive Disorder. I have outlined many of the separate components that are included within the OCD. There is one that is so large that it deserves its own chapter...THE NUMBERS!!! The numbers play a major role in the world of OCD. There are a lot of things that include numbers such as mathematics, science, accounting, construction, etc. These are all careers where numbers are used to create something. They all revolve around a particular number system. These are nothing like the Obsessive Compulsive number system. Trust me...nothing like it!

OCD is based off of its own number system. As you already know, there are "Good" numbers and "Bad" numbers. The good numbers are the number system that make you feel right or good when you perform a task for that many times. The bad numbers make you feel incorrect or bad when you do something that amount of times. There are many different number systems within the OCD. Someone might feel better doing something two times or six times. There is no rhyme or reason for this difference. Unfortunately, the only number that does not exist in the OCD number platform is one. You will never feel good just doing something once. Damn it! How great would that be?

The numbers are done in single ranges, sets and even sets of sets. For this example, I will use the number five. A single range is when you do something five times only. I call this one set. I use the plural sets to indicate when something is done in more than one set. Let's say that you did something ten times. In OCD terms, one set of five is one set, so two sets of five is two sets. In other words, if you do something ten times, that is two sets of five. Understand? If not, don't worry, just keep reading. If you do something in multiple sets, these are sets of sets. Using the same number five, let's say you did something fifteen times. That is three sets of five. Let's say you did something twenty-five times. That is five sets of five. Now remember, the OCD will continue to grow and take over. So, you will need to do your good number of sets. This means that if your good numbers are three and five, you will need to perform the task with three sets or five sets. This means that you will need to do something fifteen times or twenty-five times. Are you catching on. Fun, right?

Within the numbers of sets, there are ways to end or close a set. This means that you have another action or verbal item to split the sets. Sometimes the verbal item can be just counting the sets such as 1 set, 2 sets, 3 sets. You might have taken behavior therapy so you say "Do the behavior therapy!" or "Don't do it!" in between the sets. So, it is something like this: Do one set and say: "Do the behavior therapy!", Do another set and say: "Do the behavior therapy!", Do another set and say: "Do the behavior therapy!", Do another set and say: "Do the behavior therapy!", Do another set and say: "Do the behavior therapy!". I am sure that you see the irony? What kind of system is this? You are repeating in OCD numbers to do the behavior therapy. If you are repeating that, then you are definitely NOT doing the behavior therapy. That's for sure. What a ridiculous system. Can you believe it?

I know that by now you see how people with OCD live in numbers. Everything that they do and feel are around numbers. Let me give you a small window into what it is like to live in numbers. Let's use this example: your day. What did you do today? Now, while you are thinking of that, imagine if you had to do everything you have done in numbers. Let's examine this. Let's say you brushed your teeth. Imagine if you had to brush your teeth fifteen times or three sets of five. Did you have a cup of coffee? Now imagine you had to have three cups. Did you get dressed? Now imagine that you had to put your clothes on, take them off and put them on again. Let's say you had to do this three sets of three or nine times. Did you have your morning breakfast? Did you have to have three items or five items? Maybe you had 1 egg, 1 piece of toast and three scoops of cottage cheese. This is three items and one item had three scoops. Basically, this is one set of three and one set of five. You see how it works? Now imagine this number scheme throughout your entire life such as work, social situations, family time, etc. You have to do everything in numbers. Image what one day would be like? What one month would be like? Imagine what one year would be like? See what I mean? The bottom line is that people with OCD live in numbers. Numbers here, numbers there, numbers everywhere.

There are three types of numbers. There are compulsion numbers, force of habit numbers and, of course, random numbers. Each number pattern has its own system within itself to satisfy the OCD. Even though each type of number is different from another, they all function the same way. That is to say they all are based on your personal good and bad numbers. They function around your number scheme. They work together in the sense that they seem like one major system, but they are in fact slightly different. Either way, the numbers are troublesome.

I will start off with compulsion numbers. These are the numbers that are used to satisfy a compulsion. These numbers are the amount of times that you need to perform a certain task in order to satisfy a compulsion. In other words, to make you feel that the compulsion is actually done and completed. You will feel that you are past the obsession when the number compulsions are met. This can involve many different steps. The obsession will occur. It does not matter what the obsession is; it will call in the anxiety. The compulsion will then appear and will include a number scheme that needs to be done. This may include having to touch something, say something, do something or all of the above. The compulsion numbers can be very high and long lasting.

I will give you a few examples of the compulsion numbers. Let's say that you go into the kitchen and wash your hands and turn off the water. All of a sudden, you feel as if you did not turn the water off. You will need to check the faucet a certain compulsion number of times in order to "Feel" as if you did, in fact, turn off the faucet. This might include pushing down on the faucet in order to "Know" that you have officially turned it off. Maybe you will need to do this in sets or sets of sets. It might involve walking in and out of the kitchen a few times to separate the sets. The anxiety might raise and lower throughout the process.

Let's say that you park your car. This involves you turning it off, getting out of the car, closing the door and beeping the remote to lock it. The obsession that you did not lock your car hits. As a result, the compulsion hits as well. You will now have to beep the alarm to lock it a certain number of times. For me, I would need to lock it three or five times. Someone else might need to lock it four or eight times. The numbers will depend on your good and bad number scheme. If six is your number, you will need to relock the car door six times.

My final example of compulsion numbers has to do with the repeating. Let's say that you are in a conversation and you tell someone that you will be at their house at five pm. The second you say it, the obsession hits. The obsession will be that you did not give them a time at all. You will get anxiety that you will either be early and the person will be angry or that you will be late and that everyone will be waiting for you. So, the compulsion will hit that you will need to tell the person repeatedly that you will be there at five pm. You will need to repeat this a certain number of times. Again, if your number is three, four, five, six, etc. This is how many times you will need to repeat or "Confirm" that the correct time for you to be there is five pm. You will need to get creative with the repeating so that no one knows that you are, in fact, repeating. You might say that "I'll be there at five pm." Or "Five pm works for me." Or that "I'll see you tomorrow at five pm." Either way, the repeating will occur. This "double checking" will be the repeating compulsion and will need to be completed with the compulsion numbers. Whatever your number is, is how many times you will need to "Confirm" that the time for you to be there, is in fact, five pm.

The next type of numbers is the force of habit numbers. The force of habit numbers are just numbers that are used in everyday life. These numbers are much more relaxed. They are just the certain numbers in which you like to do things. These numbers will still fall into your personal number scheme. You just feel more comfortable doing everyday things in these numbers. These everyday things can be eating a meal, drinking, brushing your teeth, brushing your hair, checking to make sure that you have your wallet and keys, sitting down somewhere, checking all the doors and windows, etc. There are tons of everyday things that can be done in numbers.

The reality is that people do not count everything that they do. People do not know or care how many times they do a simple task like eating, drinking, sitting, going outside, walking the dog, changing the TV channels, etc. These daily tasks are not usually done in numbers. People do not count how many M and M's, how many pretzels or handful of nuts that they have. They do not count how many times they sat in a certain chair. People do not count how many times they went to the restroom or how often they used their phones. People do not count how many times they walked on one street verses another street. People do not count how many times they spoke to someone or went for a walk. People do not count how often they have a soda or a glass of water. People do not count how many scoops of cottage cheese they had for breakfast that morning or how many scoops of ice cream they had that night. People do not count how many grapes they had or bites of a banana. They do not count how many times they have been to the bathroom or entered a room. They do not count how many times they had a conversation pertaining to a certain subject. They do not count how often they checked their watch or their phone for the time. They do not count how often they roll over in bed or put their glasses on. They do not count how many times they tied their shoes or tightened their tie. They do not count how often they shook someone's hand or waived to somebody. Plain and simple: as a rule, people do not count.

Most people would not notice how many pieces of candy they had during a movie. The average person would not notice how many pieces of bread that they had with dinner or how many sips of a drink that they had. Most people do not count what they eat, drink, wear, carry, etc. To the average person, they just ate, drank, sat, talked and had candy. They don't realize how many things can be done in numbers. Let's say you give someone a bag of nuts. A while later, you go back and ask them how many handfuls of the nuts they had, they will not know. They did not count or even think of how much they consumed. Can you imagine that someone asked you "Excuse me, how many sips of that coffee have you had?" They would not know. What if someone asked you how many times you sat in that seat. What if they asked how many times you tied your shoes that particular day? What if they asked how many handfuls of popcorn you had that day? The bottom line is that nobody counts how many times they do something. They don't even think about it. If they notice, they do not even care.

People with OCD live in numbers so they tend to count a lot. These numbers do not have any consequences, anxiety or thought attached. There is no major obsession or reason for these numbers. You do not feel like something is wrong or about to happen if you disobey the number system. Like the rest of OCD, these numbers depend on the individual person and their "Comfortable" numbers. These numbers just put the person at ease. There is no rhyme or reason as to this type of counting. You just feel better doing these tiny tasks a certain amount of times. These numbers will always be your good numbers.

My first example is with eating. Let's say that I want a

snack. I will go to my cabinet and see what is there. I may decide on three items or five. I will have crackers which is one item. I will have nuts which is two items. I will add some candy as a third item. I may add a piece of bread and a slice of cheese to make it five items. You see what I mean? This is just an ordinary snack and I did it with a certain number of items. I might add more of each item, but they will still be the same amount of variety. If I add almonds as a nut, that will count for one item. If I want to add more almonds, that will be fine, because they are still considered one item.

Another example would be sort of like the first but slightly different. Let's say that I want a small handful of almonds. I go to the cabinet and just take a tiny handful. Then, a few minutes later, I would like a little more. I go to the cabinet and grab another handful. I only had one item, but I did it twice. I will need to get a third handful to complete a set of three times. See how living in numbers works?

Let's use sitting in a chair. Sounds like a typical little thing that people do on a daily basis without any further thought. But, with OCD, there is always a number. So, I go outside to sit on my patio. I have two chairs and one lounge chair. Let's say it is a warm day and I would like to sit outside for a little while before dinner. I start out by sitting in one of the chairs. I realize that I am thirsty so I get up and get a cold soda. I go back to the chair. By now, you should be up to speed on living with numbers and can guess what happens next. I sit down and now I sat in the chair twice. I would feel that I should sit in it a third time. So, needless to say, I finish my soda and get up out of the chair and go into the house and put the glass in the sink. I now realize that I sat in the chair twice and what else? You guessed it, I also went outside twice. I will need to do it one more time. So, I go back outside and sit in the chair. I then went outside three times and sat in my chair three times. This completes the fact that I did both three times each. See how the system works?

There are many examples of these types of force of habit

numbers. Let me go over a few. Let's say that I take my glasses off to clean them. I take them off and wipe them. Then I put them back on. I notice that there is a smudge on them. I then take them off, clean the smudge and put them back on. If you notice, I took them off to clean them a total of two times. So, I naturally take them off one more time, clean them and put them back on. This makes it a total of three times.

I went to visit a friend with two cats. I was about to leave so I pet one of them one time and the other one time. Then, I pet one of them another time to make it a total of three pettings. It would be much easier if they had three cats.

I went to a dinner party. We have finished dinner and it was time for dessert. There were two types of dessert. There was a pie and a cake. The host gave everyone a slice of pie and a piece of cake. If you notice, one of each is a total of two. I then had another piece of cake to make it a total of three parts of dessert. It would have been easier if there were three types of dessert.

My next example will involve the usual symptom of hand washing. Most people just go into the bathroom and wash their hands. They simply just turn on the faucet, put some soap on their hands and hold their hands under the water while scrubbing for a few seconds. That's it. For me, I prefer to wash my hands the same way, but do it three quick times. In other words, I turn on the water and tab some soap on and rinse my hands. I do this three times and that constitutes hand washing. I can do it both ways and wash my hands the exact same way that other people do, but I just "feel" better doing it in my native numbers. A simple set of three works for me.

These numbers can work anywhere. Most people brush their teeth by going over the top or bottom row and then doing the opposite. I prefer to brush the bottom teeth one time and then the top teeth two times. This is a total of three times.

Let's say that I brushed my hair. I look to see if it looks okay. I look in the bathroom mirror. I then go into the bedroom and look in that mirror. Yup, you guessed it, that was two times. So, I simply go back into the bathroom and look in it to make sure my hair looks good. This will complete the set of three times that I looked in the mirror.

I like to walk. Let's say that one of my shoes became untied. I need to tie it. I then tie my shoe. Then, I will untie and tie my other shoe twice to make it a complete set of three times. See what I mean? This is how these force of habit numbers work.

I work on a computer. I save my files three or five times. This way, I feel better. I also know that they are saved. Even writing this book, I save my files three or five times.

The force of habit numbers can be done anywhere and with anything. They are just a number scheme that makes me feel better on a daily basis. They do not cause major anxiety or an obsession. I just feel better doing them. If I don't do them, I might get a little uneasy, a tad bit of anxiety or a basic feeling of something not being done. The feelings will not be strong enough to make me do some sort of compulsion. The feeling will still be there but not last too long. I believe that an obsession appears only when not doing things the normal number of times. I don't need to react to the feelings. I just feel better doing things these certain number of times. It is just how I do things.

The final type of numbers are the "Random" numbers. The random numbers are numbers that someone with OCD just notices in everyday life. These numbers can be inside or outside. They can be within the local landscape or the inside of a home or office. These numbers are just there. There is no rhyme or reason for these numbers. It is just something that people with OCD notice. These numbers do not need to be counted in sets or sets of sets. There is no repeating, no obsession and absolutely no anxiety. There is no compulsion, no feeling and no consequence. There are no rules or regulations to these numbers. They are truly "Random" numbers.

These are everyday places and things where someone with

OCD can find numbers. I will notice that there are numbers. There are no real numbers in these places, but I will notice them anyway. It is second nature. I just notice numbers where there are no numbers. I will notice them inside or outside the house. I will notice them in my office. I will notice them in cars, planes or boats. I just tend to notice them. I can be tense or relaxed. I can be calm or upset. I can be awake or tired. I can be happy or sad. Either way, I will notice these random numbers.

These random numbers show up in all places. I usually notice them in terms of my traditional number scheme. My good numbers are three and five so I tend to notice sets of three or five.

Most people will sit on their patio and just relax. They will not notice anything unusual. They will not notice how many flowers there are, how many chairs or how many slats of wood make up their outside fence. They will not notice the different parts of a hose. They will not notice the wood beams or table legs. They will not notice the tiny details that make up a back patio.

My first example of these random numbers will be when I am relaxing at home on my own patio. I can sit there and my eyes tend to wander. I notice that there are slats of wood in my fence. I count out three of them that are next to each other. I may even count out five. See what I mean? They are truly random numbers.

Most people will sit out on their patio and see a lounge chair and think nothing of it. I notice it in random numbers. I see the actual wicker frame, the cushion on top and the pillow on top of that. I see three things put together.

I notice that there are some nice flowers. I will count out three that are together. I may notice three lemons on a nearby tree. I will notice that there are three leaves on a particular branch.

Let's take the hose for example. I notice that there is a water pipe, the hose itself and the spray nozzle. I see that as three separate parts. This makes it a complete set of three.

I look up and notice that there are beams of wood on the upstairs balcony. I count out or select three or five beams.

I see that there is a table. I notice that the table has four legs. My eyes will just connect with the numbers. I can count three of the four legs. I can also count all four legs and then another leg so it is a total of five.

I may look over my fence and notice a line of trees. I may count three of them. I may see that there are three branches on one tree. I may see it as three different color leaves and count those. Either way, it will need to be a set of three or five.

I may just notice a certain number of items out there. I may see a gas pipe, a barbeque and a planter. I will count these as I see three things.

I will notice that there are three potted plants. I will notice the amount of leaves on each plant and the number of buds that need to bloom.

My patio is tiled. I will count out three or five tiles. There is an outside rug. I will notice the pattern on the rug. It is little colored squares. I will count out three or five of the squares. I will see it in numbers. I will automatically look at three or five separate squares. There can be multiple patterns and colors. This is all in one rug. It can be separated into many different number sets. The sets can be counted many different ways.

Let's move into the house. Most people will just sit in their living room on the couch. They are doing nothing but sitting on the couch. They are not counting or seeing these numbers. They are just sitting and maybe watching TV or reading a book.

I can sit in my living room and notice many different number schemes within viewing distance. I will automatically just start to break up the room into many different number schemes and patterns. Each of these can be counted and viewed as a set or sets of numbers. There are numbers everywhere that most people don't even notice.

I can sit on the couch and notice that there are three pillows on the couch and three large cushions to sit on. I can also notice that there are three large cushions to lean on.

I can see a wood fire place and notice that there are three different patterns in the wood. I can notice that there are three different angles on the sides of the fire place. I count out three different remote controls on the top of the fireplace.

I notice that there is a wood chair that has three wood poles that make up the back of the chair. I can also count out five of them. I can count that there are two pillows and one blanket on the chair.

I look over to an end table. I see that there is one lamp and two photos. This makes up a complete set of three. You see how these numbers work?

I look at the decorative rug and notice the pattern. The pattern has different colors and shapes. I can count three or five shapes. I can notice three or five different colors. I can count out the different parts of the rug. I can notice square shapes or round. Red or blue. Artistic or plain. Either way, I break up the rug and count it into numbers.

Most people look at a simple painting and like it or hate it. They notice a lot to it. The meaning, the symbolism, the expression. I would notice that there are three or five characters. I will notice the amount of colors. I will notice the number of strokes or patterns in the characters. I will see the number of trees or the border of the frames. I will also see the number of paintings on the wall. See how this works?

The random numbers can be counted anywhere. They can be in a house, an office, a restroom, a restaurant, inside, outside, a grocery store, a plane or boat, on the ocean or on the land. The bottom line is that these random numbers are everywhere and can be counted at all times. Everything can be broken up into numbers.

The random numbers are somehow part of the OCD world. I do not know why, but they are. I will just notice numbers where no one else does. I will see them anywhere that I go in my daily life. I can see them while in my hometown or on a vacation. I can see them on a holiday or regular day. I can see them everywhere. Most people don't notice, think or care about these numbers. I notice them everywhere.

I tried my best to explain to you what it is like to live in numbers. It is not easy. The entire world is numbers. I can count or put together a number scheme anywhere and anytime. They are always in my three or five number scheme. These are my good numbers.

People with Obsessive Compulsive Disorder live in numbers. We all do. Whether the numbers are tied to a compulsion, force of habit or random. Either way, we live in numbers. Most people don't even think of these things. We live with these numbers everyday of our lives. We count in them, check in them, repeat in them and overall live in them. It can be quite exhausting. People who have OCD understand these numbers. They make sense to us. In some ways, they comfort us and in others they upset us. From the moment we wake up to the moment we go to sleep. We function with these numbers. These numbers exist in our lives whether we like it or not. We do things in numbers that most people don't even notice. Day or night, rain or snow, heat or cold. Relaxing Huh?

CHAPTER 7: FEEDING TIME!

"Come And Get It!"

The previous chapters display how Obsessive Compulsive Disorder is structured. I have shown you that there are obsessions, anxiety and compulsions. I have listed certain types or categories of the obsessions. I have listed many different types of compulsions. I have tried to show you what daily life is like when you have OCD. How we live, function and react to each moment.

I have shown you what a typical day looks like. You now know what a good day and a bad day looks like. With OCD, there are several different elements that can make it trigger in one's life. We have discussed the triggers and why they may happen. I have outlined what it is like to have OCD. Doctors and the medical community usually explain the overall logistics within the OCD brain to show you how the OCD functions. They will have the medical or scientific reasons that you have OCD. They can tell you what causes it; such as genetics or low serotonin. They will certainly be able to tell you about all of the parts of the brain in neurological terms. Most of the doctors that I have been to seem to treat the OCD as a whole. You have OCD. You have to deal with it with medication and behavior therapy. The reality is that they do not mention two major aspects. You have heard the "what" and the "why". I want to show you the "how". I want to show you "how" the OCD works. I would hope that I have a better perspective because I have it. I am not writing from a medical journal or have a fancy degree. I am not writing with major medical references. I am not writing using major medical terminology. I am not a doctor of any kind. I am just trying to explain how the OCD gets its power. How it grows. How it lowers. This might help you understand why it can take over someone's life. I want to show you "how" that actually happens. The process that takes place for it to grow. I also want to show you what it takes to lower it. I hope most people can lower it to a small or low enough level where it is manageable and livable.

Let's start off with the way the OCD grows. I want to begin with the basic premise. It grows by surrendering to it...PERIOD!!! The more you do it, the more it grows. It will just keep growing. If allowed, it will completely grow out of control. Let's examine what that means. I will walk you through some of my basic symptoms. I will lay out the way that each symptom can grow. I will show you the process of building the OCD up. I will show you why it can grow and when it will grow. Ok? Let's begin.

I will begin with the obsessions or thoughts. A thought can appear out of nowhere. It might be extremely unexpected. Sometimes with experience, you will usually know when a thought will occur as well as what the thought will be. Most of the thoughts will be either the same or the same subject matter. They are part of your usual obsessions. Anyway, the thought appears immediately. There will be under a split second where you can devalue the thought. The reality is that since it happens so fast, most people end up validating the thought. This validation is what triggers the anxiety and the compulsions.

The obsessions or thoughts will show up, leaving you with an extremely short window in which to react to it. This reaction matters. The fact of the matter is that the second, and I mean, literally the millisecond that you react to it, you have just justified the thought. You have now validated the obsession. The second the thought is validated, you now have an obsession. This obsession will last a while whether you do the compulsions or not. The instant that a thought is validated, it becomes something real. A real thought is also something that is believable or might actually happen. The second you "believe" or feel that the thought might be real or possible, the thought has power to strengthen. The second that you pay attention to it or even think about it, it will grow. The problem is that if you give it any chance, it might get worse. The second you pay any attention to the Obsessive Compulsive Disorder, you have just fed it.

Sometimes, people with OCD tend to negotiate with the thoughts. Negotiations usually begin with the first time the thought occurs. You tend to try to blow it off by saying that it is impossible or bullshit. The second you negotiate with the thoughts is when you have begun the process of growing the thoughts. Every minute you think about how fake the thoughts are, you are feeding them. Just by thinking of the possibility of the thoughts being a reality, you feed them.

An example of feeding a thought can be explained with a typical door locking obsession. As I have mentioned in earlier chapters, locking a car door can be difficult with Obsessive Compulsive Disorder. So, let's use this as an example of feeding it. I get out of my car and push the button on the keychain to lock the car. The car lights flash and the horn beeps. I start to walk away. A few seconds go by and I get a thought that I did not lock the door at all. I feel that if I do not check it, it will remain open. The thought changes to the fact that someone will definitely steal the car if it is not checked. When the thought hits, I have two choices. I can feed it or starve it. I will end up feeding it if I even think about whether or not I locked it in the first place. The second that I negotiate with the thought, I have fed it. Basically, think of the negotiating process as trying to add logic to the process. By that, I mean, trying to diffuse the thought. I can tell myself that I definitely locked the car. I can bring up the fact that I definitely heard the sound of the car horn beeping as the doors locked. I can also just say that the feeling that I did not lock the door is just an OCD obsession and is nonsensical. The reality is that even these thoughts feed the OCD. The second you negotiate or try to bring reality into it, the thought has been fed. If I begin to think about whether or not I did actually lock it, I begin feeding it. The compulsions will further the feeding process. The compulsions act as a reinforcement to the process. If you do the compulsion ONCE and only ONCE...you have reinforced the thought. The second you do anything towards feeding it, it will get stronger.

Once you feed a thought, it becomes stronger and more difficult to deal with. Think of it as a child that craves attention. This child wants power and control. If you give into the child by giving it the attention that it needs, you have reinforced the behavior. The child now knows that whenever it wants your attention, it just has to act out. The OCD acts out with thoughts and feelings. This is why, if you react to the thought, it will gain in strength. If you begin doing the compulsions. It will grow even more. Sometimes the compulsions are completed by force of habit. Even the force of habit compulsion will cause it to get stronger.

The reality of the thought does not matter. If you believe that it is real or possible, you will get anxiety. The anxiety will make the OCD even worse and more believable. The very fact that you try to diffuse it by telling yourself things like "You locked the car", "I would not have left the car without locking it" or "I live in a safe neighborhood", the more you are feeding it.

Here is another example of feeding a thought. Let's say that you are in your office at work getting ready to go home. You turn off your computer and leave. In the elevator, you get a thought that you did not actually turn off your computer. This will morph into the thought that you left your computer on and anyone can access your company's important files. You have two choices. Go back upstairs and repeatedly check it or start the negotiations. The second you say or think of things like "The computer will go to sleep soon", "No one is there as everyone went home" or "Someone would need a password to get into the important files or databases", you have now fed the thought.

Let's add one more example. I will make this an obvious

irrational thought. I will show you that trying to rationalize the thought is also feeding it. Even thinking that the thought is not real and is irrational feeds it. I will use an example involving aliens. Imagine that you have two pairs of jeans. One of the pairs is blue and the other is black. You get a feeling that if you put the blue pair on, then aliens with show up and take over the Earth. You have learned about behavior therapy and do not want to feed the OCD. So, you put on the blue pair despite the thought. While wearing the blue jeans, the thought gets a little stronger. You try to rationalize with it by saying "There is no such thing as aliens", "Aliens will not come to take over the human race because I am wearing the blue jeans", "There is no way that this thought is true". Just by reasoning with the thought and trying to prove how unreal it is, you have fed it.

The overall point is that giving the obsession ANY sort of thought or time, the OCD is fed. If you react to it, you feed it. If you get a thought with anxiety and you react to it, you feed it. If you pay any attention to the OCD at all, you feed it. If you negotiate with it or try to prove why it is irrational, you feed it. The second you feel that it is real or react as such, you feed it. If you even so much as think of whether or not to do the compulsions, you feed it. If you say that you will only do the small and easy compulsions, you feed it. See the point. By paying any attention to the thoughts or feelings at all, you feed the entire process of OCD. By giving it attention, the OCD thought will have the strength and the power and will only grow. The second you feed any portion of it, it will grow. If you feed it and it grows, the only thing you can do is a clean-up which is either dealing with the thought lingering and applying the behavior therapy or just plain doing the compulsions no matter how long or how many days they last.

I have covered the process of how the thoughts/obsessions grow. Now, let's discuss what happens after the thought is allowed to grow. There are many different types of thoughts. A lot of the thoughts are based on fears of something bad happening.

Though not all thoughts are based on fears, many are. They are based on something or an event that one is afraid of happening. Sure, you can have an obsession about winning the lottery, buying a nice house or being healthy. But, let's face it, there is no fear in that. The obsessions are based on some human fears. Some of these thoughts are fears specific to each individual person. Some of the fears are generic human fears that many people have.

A generic fear might be associated to someone who is constantly worried about their health. Maybe they work in a hospital. Another generic fear might be that you will be in a plane crash because there was a recent one. A lot of people might fear that they did something that is against God if they are brought up in a really religious family. Everybody has some sort of fear that is common.

A specific fear is a fear that only the specific individual will fear. It is basically something that is just a fear that they personally have. This can be a fear that their tooth paste might be contaminated. Maybe they have had a cold sore. They might constantly have a fear of food poisoning. Maybe they were up sick all night from some bad food at some point. Maybe they have an irrational fear of losing their job or getting fired. This could be because they have made a few mistakes at work. Maybe this person likes adrenalin sports like skydiving or parasailing. If they have OCD, they might always fear that they will get injured in an accident. You see what I mean. Each of us have different fears and reasons for having them.

The OCD takes control of these fears and uses them against the OCD sufferer. The OCD fears are not always real or rational. I can tell you that if the fear exists, it will become a large OCD issue. It will happen over and over. The OCD will use the fear and create compulsions around it. Basically, if you are afraid of getting shot...there will be a lot of compulsions that have to be done so you will not be shot. See where I'm going with this?

Once you have a fearful thought and get an obsession,

you have two choices, one is to do the compulsions and two is to ignore it. If you begin to do the compulsions, you will give the thought strength. This strength will cause the thought to become a major issue. It will be re-created over and over. It will come in different forms. If your fear is specific, it will become a usual or reoccurring obsession. Basically, once you give a thought power, you will always have it. It will become stronger and stronger and set a precedent. This precedent is where you will always need to do the compulsions whenever this same thought happens. The thought will also start to happen more often. Basically, it will become part of your arsenal of obsessions. Each person will have ten or fifteen basic issues or thoughts. These thoughts will happen monthly, daily or whenever. Once you have the arsenal set up, the OCD will use these as your usual obsessions. I know most of you probably have not heard it described this way before. But it is true. I know the fact that you have a few obsessions that will be your usual obsessions or the basic premise that you have ten or so basic thoughts that you have every day is hard to believe. It is what I have experienced in all of my years of suffering with Obsessive Compulsive Disorder. I know it still seems weird and you have probably never heard this in a medical journal. So let's go over some examples.

Let's start out with an example of a generic fear that everyone might have. I'll use cancer. Everyone is afraid of developing some sort of cancer. That is a normal and logical fear. It is one that we all can understand. We all can see why that would be such a fear. So, someone with OCD, being human, could also have this fear. The fear will occur differently with OCD. Imagine this person with OCD does not check their stove a certain number of times to make sure it is off. This person's number is five (force of habit) and they check it three and try to enlist the behavior therapy. Since they checked the stove the wrong number of times and did not finish the set, they will get the obsession that if they do not check the stove another two times, they will soon get cancer. The person might be afraid of the thought, feeling or maybe the anxiety that is attached. So, they simply check the stove another two times. They just fed the OCD. Once fed, it gets hungry so the same obsession will reoccur somewhere else in the person's life. Maybe they will brush their hair three times and not five times. The person does not brush two more times. So, guess what, the obsession will reoccur that they will get cancer. See what happened? They did not do the five compulsions on the stove. They got the cancer thought. Now the same thought occurred with the person brushing their hair. See what happens when you feed the OCD the first time? Maybe the person will drink three glasses of water and not five. Then if they stop at three, they will get the cancer obsession. See how the thoughts grow? The first time it was fed was on the stove. It grew! The second time it was fed was with brushing the hair. It grew! The third time it was fed was with the amount of water that the person drank. It grew! You see? Get the idea? If you feed any thought once, it will reoccur. This was an example of a normal fear that everyone might have. A common fear among all humans with or without OCD.

Let's examine a specific fear. Remember, a specific fear is a fear that only the one person with OCD has. I will use one of mine. I am always afraid of misspelling someone's name in written communication such as email, texts, notes, etc. I will show you how this grew. I misspelled someone's name on a greeting card one day. It was embarrassing. I worried about it over and over. So, the next time I was making out a greeting card, I got the obsession that I would misspell the person's name. I felt the need to recheck the name a certain number of times. Yup! This fed it. Then I felt that I would misspell someone's name in an email at work if I did not check and recheck it a certain number of times. Then I felt I would misspell someone's name in a text if I did not do the number compulsion on checking the spelling over and over. See what I mean? I screwed up and misspelled someone's name on a birthday card one time. I then felt that I needed to recheck the person's name. Once I checked the name,

I felt that I needed to check the name a certain amount of times. It was a simple number compulsion. I did the compulsion and checked the person's name a certain number of times. This fed the thought. It grew. I then had the exact same obsession where I needed to check all names a certain number of times to make sure they were spelled correctly in ALL written communications. It went from the greeting cards to emails and to texts. So, now whatever my current number is, I need to read the person's name a certain amount of times to make sure that I got the name spelled correctly. This, as you can see, is just a fear that is specific to me and me alone. The process of feeding the OCD and it growing is the exact same as the generic fears that everyone has. See what I mean? I fed it. It grew. The same thought spread and re- occurred in many other situations. Get the idea?

There are many different thoughts that can reoccur. The obsessions will reoccur with similar situations. Here are a few examples of how the same obsessions will reoccur. If I lock my front door once, I will get an obsession that it is not locked. I will feel that I am in danger or might get robbed. This feeling will be relieved if I lock the front door with a compulsion. If I do the compulsion, from then on, I will get that same obsession every time I need to lock a door. Any door.

If I turn off a water faucet once, I will get an obsession that the water is still running and I never actually turned the water off. I will need to turn off the faucet with a compulsion. If I do it, I will then get the same obsession of the water being on with any other water source that I need to shut off. It could be the shower or the garden hose.

If I turn my oven off once, I will get an obsession that I never actually turned the oven off. I will decide that I can get rid of this feeling by checking the oven with compulsions. If I do it, I will get the same obsession with any appliance that I need to turn off. An oven, stove, coffee pot, etc. It will reoccur with every type of appliance that I need to turn off.

Now you know how the obsessions and thoughts are fed and how they grow. The obsessions will show up here and there. If you feed them, they will reoccur all over the place. The will grow in strength and power. Then they will end up everwhere. You will have the same thought reoccur multiple times in everything. The thoughts will become your common thoughts. They will reoccur and end up as part of your specific obsessions. Your specific obsessions will happen in different places, times and have different compulsions. The different places and compulsions might change, but the fearful obsession will remain the same. I am sure a lot of people with OCD have certain sets of reoccurring obsessions that will be the same and constantly happen. Once the thought or obsession is fed. It will grow and grow and grow.

I have explained how the obsessions and thoughts get their power. I will now explain how the compulsions grow. The compulsions are fed the same way. The process will seem the same. All right, you got me! It is the exact same. The obsessions and compulsions go hand in hand. Hey, there is a reason it is called Obsessive Compulsive Disorder. Anyway, the prior paragraph was from the side of the Obsessions. How you give them power, feed them and how they grow. This section is from the side of the compulsions. The compulsions are a method used by the OCD to feed it so it can grow. I will show you how the compulsions are used and how they grow. The compulsions are the true form or food for the OCD. It is "How" the thought gets power. It is "How" you feed the thought. The compulsions are how you feed the OCD simply by doing them. Once you perform a compulsion, the OCD is fed. That is the "Food" of the OCD. The point being is that when I use the term "Bad" to describe a day with OCD, I am talking about the compulsions. For me, a bad day is a day spend entirely on compulsions and numbers. Repeating and checking. Touching and looking. All in the sets and numbers that feel comfortable to me. When the OCD skyrockets, the compulsions take over and you end up doing them over and over and over. It can be a VERY difficult day.

The compulsions are designed to "GET RID" of the thought. They are used to "RELIEVE" the anxiety or the thought. By the way, they don't do either. The point is that people with OCD get trained early on that the compulsions are the key to life. Once you do the compulsions, everything will be fine. The compulsions are the vehicle to rid your brain of a painful or fearful thought. They are used to get you out of living in a set of numbers. They are used to cancel out the horrific thoughts that you may be having.

The truth is that the compulsions are the thing that feed the OCD the most. They allow it to grow. They allow it to multiply all over one's life. The compulsions are the physical acts that someone with OCD does in order to relieve them of the thought. These physical things can be done in numbers and sets of numbers. They can be done in a certain order. They can be completed in one day or over many days. They can even be altered to a specific event or place. The one thing that all the compulsions have in common is that they can be done anywhere, anytime or any place. The OCD will use them everywhere. They will occur everywhere. They will occur every day. They will occur with each and every thought. The truth is that is how they grow. They can be done anywhere, anytime or any place. They can be done physically. They can be done mentally. They can be done aloud or in your head. They can be done no matter what. If you are awake, they can be done.

The problem with the compulsions is that they grow so easily. The point being that if they can be done in one place, then why not another? If they can be done in one set, then why not another? If they can be done with one person, then why not another? If you can do them out loud, then why not do them while whispering under your breath secretly? If you can do them with your Mother, then why not other family and friends? If you can do them in your car, then why not an elevator or a plane? If they show up at night, then why not during the day? If you can do them on a Monday, then why not a Wednesday? You see what I mean?

The compulsions grow by doing them or reacting to the OCD. It does not matter whether they are force of habit or include an obsession or irrational thought. Either way, if you do them, they will grow and grow. They will get larger and larger and last longer and longer.

The same type of compulsion will attach to the same obsession. It will grow with the compulsions that are done. Just like the numbers, if you give the OCD any power at all, it will grow. This means that when you get a thought and do the compulsion, you have given it power. If you negotiate with the thought or compulsion in any way, you will feed the OCD. These negotiations are similar to negotiating with the numbers. This means that when you get an obsession and feel like you need to do a compulsion, you have two choices: Do the compulsion or sit through the obsessive thought. By sitting there and thinking about whether or not to do the compulsion, this becomes a type of negotiation. It will give the OCD power. Should you do the compulsion or practice CBT? The OCD will usually win in this scenario. On that happy note, let's look at some examples.

I will start with the numbers. Let's say that your "Good" numbers are three or five. This means that everything you do should be done in these numbers. They don't actually need to be done in these numbers, but with OCD, you just "Feel" better if they are. The problem with this is that you are feeding the OCD by living in the number scheme. This is how the numbers grow.

If you eat a cookie and feel that you need to eat three or five cookies, you may do it. If you do eat the "Correct" amount of cookies, you will feed the OCD. If you wash your hands and feel that you need to wash them three times, and do it, then you will feed the OCD. The numbers grow the second you do anything the "Right" number of times. Once you start doing things the "Right" or "Correct" number of times, this feeds the number system. Then the numbers will spread. They will spread from one thing to another. If you feel that you need to talk about one subject three times. Then why not another subject. Then another and another. The reality is that, just like the obsessions, if you give them any attention or do something in the number scheme, it will feed them and they will grow.

There are two ways to give the numbers their power. The first is doing something the "Right" number of times. The second is purposely doing something so the task does not end on the "Wrong" number of times. The second you think of any of this or react to it, you have just given the numbers their power and strength. The second the numbers get their strength, they will grow and begin to happen with other things. Here are some examples.

Let's say it is a day where you are talking in numbers. I may be talking to someone about my car. Then I feel that I need to say three sentences about my car. If I do the three sentences, I have just given the power to the numbers. A few minutes or hours later, I may be talking to someone about my house. Then, I will feel that I need to mention three sentences about my house. See what just happened? I did the compulsion and mentioned the three sentences about my car. By doing it, I fed the numbers. Then, I soon had to mention three sentences about my house. If I do it, I once again fed the numbers. Now I feel that the numbers are real. I will feel that when they happen, I need to do the compulsion. Once you cement or "Feel" the fact that the compulsions need to be done, the feelings will get stronger. The stronger the feelings get, the harder it will be not to do the compulsions. Once the compulsions are done a few times, the thoughts and feeling will begin when the compulsions are not completed. Now you will get anxiety if the compulsion numbers are not met. You might get an obsession if the numbers are not done correctly. You might have a lingering feeling that something is not done or finished if the compulsions are not completed. The basic point is that when the numbers are fed, they will continue and multiply. Here are some examples of how the numbers will grow when they are fed.

I will use another example of talking in numbers. I might be talking to a friend about a trip we are taking. I will get a feeling that I need say three different sentences or things about the flight. I do it and feed the OCD. The conversation with my friend continues. I mention the hotel. Now I feel that I need to say three sentences about the hotel. You see how that happened? I said three sentences about the flight, and since I did the compulsion, I now feel that I need to say three sentences about the hotel. You see how the numbers grew? I will continue to talk to my friend about our trip. Then, later in the conversation, I will feel like I need to say three sentences about the weather where we are going. You see what I mean? I felt for the first time that I needed to say three sentences about one thing. I did it, fed the OCD and it grew. I gave the OCD the power and strength. Now it grew. I started out feeling that I needed to talk about the flight in three sentences. Then it was fed, grew and took its hunger to other subjects. Then I did the compulsion and then I needed to talk about the hotel in three sentences. I fed it again and now I need to mention the weather in three sentences. By doing it the first time, I fed it. You see how it grows when fed? Did you catch how it gets hungrier? This will keep growing and growing. It will keep multiplying and multiplying. It will keep happening and happening. Pretty soon, I will need to talk in numbers over any conversation. On a bad day, it might happen with every conversation I have. This happens all because it was fed the first time.

Here is another example of how the numbers grow. Let's use the number three. If you are in the bathroom and you wash your face. Let's say that you feel like washing your face three times. So, since you are used to the OCD, you naturally do it. You washed your face three times. Now, the numbers grow so you start to brush your teeth and now you feel that you need to brush your teeth three times. Then you will feel that you need to brush your hair three times. See how it grows all over the place?

Think of it this way, if you feel that you need to wash your hands three times in the bathroom sink, then why not three times in the kitchen sink? Let's take it even further, then why not three times at your job, in restaurants, at friend's houses, etc. See what I mean? The numbers will go from one thing to another. There will be no end in sight.

This process starts out with a few numbers that you are comfortable with. Once you begin doing things in these comfortable numbers, you have given the OCD power. This will result in you feeling that more and more things need to be done in this comfortable number scheme. These numbers will just grow from one thing to another. Let's say you have to eat in numbers. Then you will have to shower in numbers. Then, why not read in numbers. You see what I mean? The numbers will jump from one thing to another. Once this happens, the numbers will blow up and be interlaced with everything. There will become a point where the numbers have grown so much that there is nothing that you can do without feeling the number amount needs to be met. No matter what the task is, you will feel that it needs to be done a certain number of times. You will feel the good numbers and bad numbers everywhere.

The numbers will exist and be applied to repeating, checking, visualizing things, talking, reading, eating, snacking, emailing, texting, taking photographs, weighing yourself, locking doors, checking ovens, cooking, cleaning, getting dressed, showering, drinking, exercising, walking, shopping, talking to friends, family, dating, traveling, lying in bed, flossing, getting gas, going in and out of doors, looking at something, walking through a mall, walking in a city, etc. The OCD has now gone EVERYWHERE!!! I really mean everywhere and in everything. Nice and fun, right?

The sets grow just like the numbers. Like the numbers, the sets might be a reaction to an obsession or irrational thought or just be a force of habit. This will keep you doing multiple sets.

The sets can be done quickly or slowly. I usually do the sets quickly when I am in public and slower when I am home. Either way, the urge to get them done and get past the entire process will linger until you complete the sets needed. The process is based on the numbers. Let's say that your "Good" numbers are three and five. The sets grow by simply doing them. The second you do them or think about doing them, the OCD is fed and the sets will grow. All it takes is for you to do one simple set and the OCD was fed. Period! Let's look at a few examples.

My first example is with a simple repeating compulsion. This is an example of repeating on myself. There is no one else involved. Here is how it works. I will use planning my errands for this example. Imagine I need to get a birthday card. Sounds simple, right? I am sitting on the couch having my morning coffee. I am thinking about what I need to do that day. I remember that I need to get the birthday card. I say this one time. "I need to get the birthday card". I immediately get a feeling that I did not say anything about the card. I know that I did, but I feel like I did not mention the card. Then, I get a light feeling that I need to repeat it. Remember, I already said it once.

Since my good numbers are three and five, I need to say it five times. So, there are four times to go to complete the number five. I simply repeat it the four more times. "I need to get the birthday card". "I need to get the birthday card". "I need to get the birthday card". "I need to get the birthday card".

As you remember, I said it five times. By doing this and giving into the feeling that I did not say anything, I completely fed the OCD. I put out a huge plate of food and fed it. Now, a few minutes will go by. I will feel that by saying "I need to get the birthday card" five times, it equals one set. You see how that works? My numbers are three and five. I said something five times and fed the OCD. Now, my OCD makes me feel that the five times is equal to one set. Can you believe it? I said something five times and only got credit for one set. I feel that each of the times

I said it, though it is really five separate times, counts as only one set. Let's count them out. I said it one time, two times, three times, four times and five times. I already fed the OCD by doing it a second time. The first time I got the feeling that I did not say it. I began negotiating with the OCD. I start to think about how I know I said it. I heard myself say it. I don't care if I did not say it. By negotiating with it, I fed it. I gave the OCD power. I have just made it stronger. This is ridiculous, right? It's just a birthday card. Hey, I might not even like the person that I am getting the card for. It happens, right? We have all been there.

Anyway, now, I am into the sets. I also get a feeling that there are more sets to be done. I have an uncomfortable feeling that I need to repeat about the birthday card another set. Remember that each set consists of repeating about the birthday card a certain number of times. Now, you already know that by reading this chapter that the simple fact that I am thinking about the sets feeds the OCD. Since I have fed it, I will have the uncomfortable feeling that I need to do the compulsion by saying it in another set.

I have a few more sips of my morning coffee and the light nervous feeling that something is not completed begins to linger. I try a little behavior therapy. I say out loud "I'm not doing it!". Sometimes, when you cut off the set forcefully, you break up the set. You can use a forceful sentence to break up and end the set. You feel like it is over as the nervous feeling of something being incomplete goes away. There is one problem with this. It becomes part of the set. Didn't see that coming did you? For some reason, the set simply includes that sentence used to "Break Up" the set into the set. It will now become part of the compulsion. If you are like me, that makes absolutely no sense. I have no idea why this happens. Go figure.

I take a few more sips of coffee. A few seconds go by and the nervous feeling comes back. It is light but still annoying. It continues to linger. I decide to just do it. I repeat another set of five and include the sentence to break up and end the set. "I need to get the birthday card". "I need to get the birthday card". "I need to get the birthday card". "I need to get the birthday card". "I need to get the birthday card". "I am not doing it!". By doing the compulsion, I just fed the OCD even more. I just gave it more power and strength. As you can tell, I don't relax much having my morning coffee.

As you can guess, the slight nervous feeling that something is incomplete shows up again. I already did two complete sets. I fed the OCD with both. The nervous feeling returns. I, once again, feel like doing the compulsion. I know that I will feel that I need to do it three or five times. I just do it a full set of five. This means three more sets of repeating about the birthday card five times and adding the sentence to break up the set. As you guessed by now, it does not break up anything. Here we go. "I need to get the birthday card". "I need to get the birthday card". "I need to get the birthday card". "I need to get the birthday card". "I need to get the birthday card". "I am not doing it!". "I need to get the birthday card". "I need to get the birthday card". "I need to get the birthday card". "I need to get the birthday card". "I am not doing it!". "I need to get the birthday card". "I need to get the birthday card". "I need to get the birthday card". "I need to get the birthday card". "I am not doing it!".

I did the complete compulsion of five sets. It should be over, right? I did the compulsions correctly. I did them in proper order. I did them exactly how I usually do them. So, what's the problem. Well, the problem is that I fed the obsessive-compulsive disorder so much that it will just keep growing. Having said that, a few minutes later, the OCD grows a little more. Now I feel that all five sets that I just completed is actually just one set. Can you believe it?

I sit on the couch and finally finish my morning coffee. I get a feeling that all five sets are only one big set. This was one big set on the couch. By doing it all on the couch, I only did one set in one place. For some reason, my OCD makes me feel that the couch counts as one location. The entire five sets of five times only counts as one set in one place. See what I mean? When you feed the OCD or give it power and strength, it will just grow and grow and grow out of control. Since I only did it in one place and the OCD works on numbers, there will certainly be many more sets that need to be completed. Basically, the OCD will take the ball and run. It will just grow each time you feed it. Yup, it's time for a second set.

I get the feeling that I need to go into a different room in the house and repeat the second set. Remember, the OCD is irrational. For some reason, my brain makes up rules that are not even real. For some reason, I feel that if I go into another room, that breaks up the sets. My brain tells me that I need to break up the sets into different rooms of the house. It makes no sense whatsoever. How does a room change break up the set? Who knows. It makes no sense to me.

I fed the OCD and the feeling of being unconformable by doing the first five sets on the couch. The feeling that something is not done or incomplete returns. I know that the quicker I get the second set done, the quicker the feeling of uncomfortable incompleteness will go away. So, needless to say, I went into the bedroom. I completed another set of repeating in the bedroom. This was not a big set. I only had to say it five single times. For some reason, that small amount counts as one set. The reason you don't have to do this five sets of five is because I switched rooms. The basic idea is that by switching the rooms, I need to just do it one quick set in each place. That will account for a completely different set. By doing this, I just fed the OCD even more. I did the compulsion. It is done right? Wrong!

I know have fed the OCD multiple times. First when I said it the first five sets on the couch. The second by going into the bedroom and completing the smaller set. I also have fed it by thinking in between about whether or not I said it and whether or not I should do the compulsions. Now, due to the recent feedings, the OCD gets power and strength. Naturally I get the same uncomfortable incomplete feeling. It feels like something needs to be done or something is not done. I am sitting in it and negotiating with it and thinking about whether or not I should force myself to use the behavior therapy. I think how ridiculous this entire process is. I feed the OCD even more. Then, I feel that I need to complete a third small set.

I already used the couch for the first set and the bedroom for the second set. I now know that I will end up doing it five sets. I will break up the sets by changing to a different room each time I do a set. This is how the OCD grows. So, needless to say, it's time to feed it even more. I do three more sets. I repeat about the birthday card in sets of five. I already did two so I need three more. I do a set in the kitchen, a set in the bathroom and another set on the couch. Let's do a quick math review. I repeated about a birthday card in five sets in five places. Not all of the sets were the same amount. Basically I may have repeated about the birthday card forty-five times. I fed it each and every step along the way. This is by actually doing it, by just thinking about doing it or by merely thinking about using the behavior therapy. See how it gets fed?

Are you ready for this? You're sure? Get this! The five sets in five places should have been enough for the OCD, right? It seems like enough. As I was doing all the repeating, it felt like it was enough. SURPRISE!!! It was not enough. Now that I fed the OCD so much and given it all that power and strength, it grows even more. Remember when I did the five sets on the couch. Then I felt like all of those sets were just one set because I did them all while sitting on the couch. The couch was just one place. Well, since I fed it by doing it five sets of compulsions in five different rooms, I now get a feeling from the OCD that all of this was in fact just one set. Yup, that's right. You read it correctly. All of that constant repeating took a long time and a lot of energy. I did it five sets of five in one place. I did it five times in four other places. My brain and the OCD now makes me feel that I just did it one giant set. This is because, even with all the constant repeating, I was in one place, my house. So, all of that crap was just one single place. So, you know where this is going. I fed it and fed it and fed it some more. It grew and grew. It will continue to grow. It will continue to grow until it is completely out of control.

Here is the next step. I did the one set in the house. I now get that funny nervous feeling that something is not complete. I feel like something is not right. I now get a thought that I need to do it a second giant set in another place. I did it inside the house for the first location. I need to go outside onto the patio and do another set. This is because the inside of the house and the outside of the house are two different places. The OCD logic dictates that two separate places are two separate sets. But I can now go back into the house again and the OCD will treat it as a third place. Back on the patio will be a fourth place, etc. The thought of the birthday card now means nothing. Now it gets into the numbers and the sets. It is all about the numbers and compulsions now. The actual initial thought of the birthday card errand means absolutely nothing. I no longer care about the birthday card. I now have to just comply with the OCD and its rules.

I know I should not be doing it as I am feeding it. I know that by doing it, I am giving it the power and strength. I know that it will just keep growing and growing because I am doing it. But I still end up just doing it and ending the entire process. Then I can move on with my day.

I remember that all of this started by remembering that I needed a birthday card. I figure that I will just go and get it. It will give me a chance to feed the OCD by doing the final three sets. I go back inside and get ready. As I am putting on my shoes and socks, I repeat a quick set of five. This completes the third place or set. Do you see how doing the compulsions just keeps it growing?

I get into my car. I drive down to the store and pick out a birthday card. I leave the store and begin to drive home. I figure that since I am alone in my car I might as well do another set. If you notice, I got the card so the errand is done. I still feel that I have to do it two more sets in two more places to complete all five sets. I pull over and do a quick set of five in my car on the way home.

I get home and park my car. I still have one other set. The feeling to complete it is still there. Remember, the first set was a large number. The second, third and fourth were quick. The final set might be longer as I want to make sure that I did the set completely. So, I choose to do it with no numbers. I just use the fact that being out of my car and outside will constitute a fifth and final set. I constantly repeat from my car to my house. I do it repeatedly and rapidly. I get into my house and it is done. I did the full five sets. I still have a little anxiety even though the entire process is over. Or is it?

A little while later, I get the feeling that I still need to do a few more sets. I do not as I ended up doing it in five places. If I do it just one more time, I will have done it six times and that is not a good number. I also know that if I continue to do it, it will jump and grow into numbers that are horrible. I will need to do it ten sets in ten different places. I decide to wait it out. Now, the OCD makes me feel like the entire day was just one single day. I feel like I need to do it again tomorrow. This will break it up by doing it two days. So, I say to myself that I will continue it tomorrow. This helps me because I will not need to do it anymore today. I can just wait until tomorrow and complete the entire compulsion. I continue on with my night. I put on the TV and start to relax.

The next morning, I wake up. I have my morning coffee. I remember that I need to complete the set from the day before. Remember what I said, that even if you think about doing it or not doing it; that "should I or shouldn't I" phase is negotiating with it. The OCD will just get stronger and stronger from that. You feed it each time you contemplate whether to do it or not. So, once again, I fed it.

I feel that I need to do the compulsions the second day too. The second day it can be the same as the first or sometimes they can be done differently. So, I just figure that I do not want to do the full set of five places as I did the first day. I will do a smaller or condensed version. As long as I do something for the birthday card repeating compulsion the second day, it will count. So, I decide to do it just two sets. I do one set out on the patio. Then I wait a little while so that the sets feel separate. If I did them back to back, the feeling would be that they were one large set. I then would need to add another set.

I wait a little while. I then do another set inside the house. I did five sets the first day and two sets the second day. This is a total of seven sets. The number seven is a good number.

I spent two days repeating over and over while paying attention to a system of rules that are not even real. I spent two days out of my life repeating over and over about a birthday card. I just had to buy a birthday card. A simple errand took two days out of my life. I repeated too many times to count. It is awful and I am exhausted. You see how the system works?

The repeating grows in many different ways. There are some times where you will feel that you did not say anything. This will happen no matter how many times something is said. You can do the entire compulsion and feel like you did not say anything. There are many different variations of this. Sometimes I feel that I did not say the entire sentence. Sometimes I feel that I did not say all or part of the sentence. Using my prior birthday card example, I might feel that I did not say the specific word "Birthday" or maybe the word "Card". I may feel that I did not say the beginning, middle or end of the sentence. If I am repeating a list of three items, I might feel that I did not say the second or third item. I may feel that the middle sentence was not said. Maybe I feel that I did not end the sentence correctly. It may feel like I said it weirdly or mispronounced the sentences. It needs to be said perfectly and in its entirety. You need to repeat it exactly the same way each and every repetition or compulsion. This feeling of imperfection is why and how the repeating continues. By giving into the feeling, you feed the OCD. Then it grows and grows. It grows into more sets, higher numbers and more places.

I want to talk about checking things in our daily life. The entire world does some form of checking. It is perfectly normal and human. Most people just check once or, at most, double check something. This double checking probably lasts under a second. Basically, if they don't remember that they turned off the stove; they might just double check to make sure the stove is off. They walk into the kitchen and look at the stove. Maybe they touch the dials or control panel to see that the stove is, in fact, off. Then they can go about their day without so much as a thought about it. The same person might turn off their car. They get out and lock the door. Maybe they were on the phone so they were slightly distracted. They finish their conversation and end their call. They might think that they don't remember locking the car. They walk back to the car and check it once. They are done. The same person might be thinking about something while walking out the front door. They were distracted so they do not remember whether or not they locked the front door. They think that they are unsure. They will then check the front door once and move on. This does not work the same way when you have Obsessive Compulsive Disorder. I, just like everybody else, have the same feelings that I forgot to turn off the stove or oven. Hey, we all do it, right?

There is one major difference, I have OCD. This makes this a very different process. Let me walk you through it. Imagine that I have just boiled some pasta on the stove. After the pasta cooks, I take it off the stove. I turn the stove off. I know that I did because I watched my hand physically turn the stove knob to the "OFF" position. I pour the pasta out of the pot and into a bowl. I begin to leave the kitchen.

A few milliseconds go by and an obsession hits. The obsession is a thought and visual of the stove still being on. I have the usual two choices. One to feed it and two to sit with the thought. I sit for a minute and the thought gets worse. It begins to linger. I feel that uncomfortable feeling that something is incomplete. I feel that I left the stove on. If the stove is left on, it might start a fire. It is unsafe. So, I figure to just feed it. I go back into the kitchen and double check the dial on the stove. I do it a quick set of five. I also touch the dial each time. This is to ensure that the stove dial is actually off. The feeling will be that it looks off, but is broken or turned wrong. This would mean that the stove is actually still on. I basically turn the dial to the off position in a set of five times. I now have fed the OCD obsession. This means that I reacted to it and gave it the power to bother me. I did the compulsion. It was fast and easy, but I still did it. Let me show you what happens next. I want to let you know how the obsession grows when it is fed. It will also become a common or usual obsession.

I used the stove to show how the obsession works. Having fed it, it will reoccur. Here is an example of that. I used the stove and felt that I needed to check the dials in order to make sure that it is off. Let's say a few days go by. Now, I use the oven. I bake some chicken in the oven. After it is cooked, I take it out and turn off the oven. I know for a fact that I turned the oven off because I saw myself turn it off. I now try to leave the kitchen. I get the same obsession. It is the feeling that the oven is still on. I feel that it is dangerous and might cause a fire. I even get a visual of it being on or smoke coming out of it. I try to sit with it. As usual, it begins to annoy me and linger. I feel the same uncomfortable feeling. I go back into the kitchen and do a quick compulsion on the oven. I check and re-check the oven dial to make sure it is off. I check it five times. I also check the oven door in a set of five to make sure that it is closed. The point is that I fed it the first time with the stove and now I got the same obsession with the oven. It is the same feeling that the appliance is still on and may cause damage or a fire. I feel that it is dangerous. The first time I got the obsession, I fed it by reacting to it and feeding it. The exact same obsession showed up with the oven a few days later. It is a different day and a different appliance, but the same obsession. I also feed it the same way but I don't know if that even matters or has anything to do with it. You see how the system works and grows? It happened two different days, with two different appliances. See what I mean? The OCD will use the same obsession over and over if you keep feeding it.

These examples were with my own appliances in my own house. The truth of the matter is that you will have that same obsession with any type of appliance. It can happen at home, or a friend or family's home. If I cook in someone's house and turn off an appliance, I will get the same obsession. It will happen all because I fed it in my home with my appliances. The obsession is not attached to a specific appliance or location, but any appliance in any location. The fact that you fed it will keep it going. The more you do the compulsions, the longer it will stay. It will reoccur over and over. It will become a usual obsession. Are you drinking yet? Let's move on.

Now, let me explain how it grows when it is fed by a simple force of habit compulsion. As you know, a force of habit compulsion is just a certain way of doing something. It includes the numbers but does not start with an obsession. The way that the force of habit compulsions grow is by doing them. Once you do them, you can not stop. If you do the compulsion for a few days or months, you will set a precedent. If and when you try to stop or use the behavior therapy, then an obsession will occur. The obsession is so that you continue to do the force of habit compulsions. Let's look at a few examples.

Let's say that I wash my hands in the bathroom. I turn the bathroom faucet off. I check the faucet three times. I do not get a thought or feeling. I just use the numbers and turn the bathroom faucet off three times. The next time I use the bathroom faucet, I again check it three times. I do this for a few days or weeks. Then, it sets a precedent. No matter what, I will always check the bathroom faucet three times. There is no thought or obsession. I just do it three times every time. This precedent will last forever. No matter how long I live in that house, I will always check the bathroom faucet three times. If you remember, I mentioned this before. The prior paragraphs describe how the OCD will grow by doing the same compulsion with different faucets. This is important. The reason is because the force of habit compulsion grows just by consistently doing it. The fact that I always wash my hands in the bathroom and check that specific faucet three times is what matters. Here is why. As you do it, you feed the OCD. By feeding the OCD, you will set a precedent. This precedent will continue forever. The point is that, since you fed the OCD, you will not be able to stop the force of habit compulsion. If you try to stop it, you will then get an obsession or the uncomfortable feeling that something is wrong. See how that works? You do the compulsions with no feelings, but if you try to stop the force of habit, then the obsession or feeling occurs. They are secondary. This is the difference. The usual way is for the obsession to happen first and then release by doing the compulsions. Basically, the force of habit is different because you do not do the compulsions to stop an obsession. You do the force of habit to avoid an obsession. See the difference? By continuing the force of habit compulsions and avoiding an obsession or feelings, you are feeding the OCD. This is how the OCD gains the strength and power with a force of habit compulsion. See how it works?

I will use an example of three different doors. As you remember, I mentioned how the OCD grows when you get an irrational thought or obsession. This is different: the force of habit grows by continuing to do the compulsion. I will use this example. Let's say I come home and close my front door. I check the front door three times on Monday. I do this by touching the front door lock three times. I continue to check the front door three times every time I come home. I do this on Monday, Tuesday, Wednesday, Thursday and Friday. I do not have a thought or feeling. I just do it this way. After a few days or weeks go by.

It becomes a force of habit to always check the front door three times. Now, as you remember, I mentioned that a thought will transfer from the front door to the back door and over to other doors. The force of habit compulsion is different. The way that this type of compulsion works is by continuously doing things a certain way. Here is what I mean. Let's say that I want to break the force of habit compulsion. I choose not to do the compulsion on the back door or any other door. I check them one time or two times at the maximum. However, the front door compulsion remains. I continue to check the front door and ONLY the front door three times. After a little while, the force of habit compulsions on the back door will not exist. The compulsion will not exist on any other door. The only door that the compulsions will exist it the front door. The front door will be the only door that I check three times. If I live in the same house for twenty years, I will ALWAYS check the front door in a set of three. I will always close it and then touch the door lock three times to make sure it is locked. You see what I mean? The force of habit compulsions will always exist wherever you continuously do them. They will never go away. If you try to stop doing them, you will immediately get an obsession or feeling that something is not right. See how the OCD jumps in with these force of habit compulsions? They do not so much grow but they stay forever. The reason this is so important is because the OCD nibbles off of these force of habit situations. Interesting right?

The force of habit compulsions feed the OCD in a different way. A more calm and passive way. The simple fact that you continue to do them, is how you feed the OCD. This will cause the force of habit compulsion to stay for a long time. The way that the force of habit compulsions grows is by doing more and more of them. Let's use my example with the front door. If you always check the front door three times and do not have any problem with any other door, that compulsion will stay. So, now let's say that you develop more force of habit compulsions. Let's say that develop a force of habit with the kitchen sink. The car, the oven, the shower, etc. See what I mean?

The force of habit compulsions feed the OCD by developing more than one. If you have ten things in your house; that is ten things in your house that you will always do a force of habit compulsion with. By continuing to do them, you feed the OCD. The number of force of habit compulsions that you have will always continue to grow. If you drink three or five glasses of water each night, you will always need to drink three or five glasses of water each night. If you drink two or six, you will feel like something is incomplete. You might even get anxiety. Same goes for the number of pretzels you have or pieces of chocolate. Some people have a nightly routine. This is where they will do the same things in the same order every night. These routines usually include eating dinner, brushing teeth or preparing clothes for the next day of work. Force of habit compulsions will develop and function exactly like a nightly routine. It will look like this: you check the front door, you check the kitchen faucet, you drink five glasses of water. See how it works?

The force of habit compulsions grows in numbers. You will have one force of habit and then another and another. Pretty soon, you will have a large number of force of habit compulsions that need to be completed each day. By doing all of them exactly the way the OCD requires, they will all stay. You will need to do them each and every time. Each and every day. Each and every year. They will never end. If you try to do them differently, you will be met with resistance. If you try to stop or change the way you do these force of habits, you will get an obsession or anxious feeling. It will come after the fact. A secondary reaction. It will come after you try to stop the usual behavior. The bottom line is that the second you try to break the force of habit behavior; you might get an obsession or feeling of anxiety or that something is not done correctly. See how it works?

You learn from experience that you will not feel right if you try to stop these things. So, you feed the OCD over and over. Day in and day out. This will just keep the force of habit compulsions going. These grow and take over by developing more force of habit compulsions. You have one, then two and on and on. Imagine how long it would take for you to have to do fifty force of habit compulsions a day? One or two is annoying. By continuing to constantly do them, they will grow to every area of your life. What starts with checking the door three time will end up doing many things a certain amount of times. Plain and simple, they grow by developing more and more things that need to be done with a force of habit compulsion. Before you know it, you will need to drink a certain number of glasses of water each night, turn lights off a certain number of times, get dressed a certain way, shower a certain way and so on. They are each quick and small on their own. Once you continue to do them, you will develop more and more and even more. Pretty soon, you will spend your entire day completing force of habit compulsions. They grow by simply and consistently doing them. Playing by the rules. The more force of habits you do, the more you will have or create. They will never end. See what I mean?

They are so easy. The numbers are usually very small. The compulsions are usually quick to do. This makes them harder to break. The idea is that why get a thought if the number is so low that it is easier to just do it. That is what makes it hard to break. Instead of sitting with the uncomfortable or uneasy feeling, just do a quick set and move on. I also think that, with OCD, you tend to just do the small ones as they are much easier to just do and get past. Imagine if you checked your front door three times. If you touch the lock three times and avoid an obsession and anxiety, isn't it just easier to do the compulsion and move on? The problem is that this is how you feed the OCD. Then you apply the same logic to another and another. Pretty soon, you are doing fifty small things a day. You end up in the force of habit pattern. This is where you do not want to fight the OCD. You tend to only fight the OCD with the really bad thoughts that have high numbers or compulsions to do. You are usually only willing to fight the thoughts that come with a large amount of high anxiety. So when you get a small tiny quick compulsion, you just do it and move on. The problem is that you end up in the pattern where you do not want to fight it. You know that you have been doing them for such a long time, that you do not want to fight the OCD. So, you just do them each and every day. These force of habit compulsions will never end. They will just keep going on and on. They are all very small, but they add up. If you have to do one thing three times, it is not so bad. When you have to do fifty things three times each, it is a pain. It can take all day. You may spend your entire day doing these compulsions. The bottom line is that if you do one thing a certain way, you might create a force of habit. If this happens, you will always need to do that one thing the same way. That will become a force of habit and the way you will need to do that one thing forever. Are you getting the way the system works?

I do not have the cleanliness issues. I am sure that they grow the same way. I am sure if you touch something and feel that you have a disease; you will do the compulsion to feed it. I am sure that you will touch something else and feel that you have the same disease. I am sure it grows the same way. I bet all of the OCD symptoms grow the same exact way. You feed it and they grow. I am sure that this goes for all of the OCD symptoms. The basic way to look at all of these issues is how many compulsions do you want to do? If you want to do compulsions each and every day, that option is available. The OCD will be happy to oblige. By doing the compulsions, you are letting it live. You are growing it. It will take over your entire life and energy by consuming your every waking moment. IT GROWS BY DOING IT... PERIOD!!!

The final thoughts that I have on how the OCD grows is the way you deal with it. The second you feed it, you have just given it the strength and power that it needs to grow. It grows every time it is fed. If you do any of the compulsions or even think about not doing them...you will feed it. If you try to purposely do something a different way or alter the compulsion...

you will feed it. Do you see how busy your day can be?

Now you understand how each section of the OCD or type of compulsion grows. The OCD will completely take over a person's life. It will be completely out of control, unstoppable and horribly painful to deal with each and every minute. It will literally be EVERYWHERE!!! It will literally be in EVERYTHING!!! The bottom line is this: If you feed it…it will grow. If it grows…it will keep growing.

CHAPTER 8: I'M SORRY!

"I Apologize That You Even Had
To Read This Chapter!"

There are many social nuances that are part of one's life. These occurrences happen during the day or night. They happen during the week, on the weekend or even during a holiday. They can happen at home, in an office, at a dinner party or other gathering. They are little social things. They happen when you are talking to someone else. They are usually so little that they can go completely unnoticed. There are things which bother us and things that do not. They are a part of basic human nature. They are the things that happen when we interact with other people through conversations, dialogues and speeches.

We communicate with other people to express ourselves. We express anger, happiness, humor, love, sadness, etc. Sometimes, the conversation can go very well and other times, not so great. Through this, we all have learned that sometimes we can say something that is not nice or can be hurtful to another person. We can say something that is not socially acceptable. We can also express happiness and joy. These interactions happen in simple conversation. We make an off color or bad joke. We make a negative comment about something. We feel grateful for someone's selfless actions. Maybe someone gave us a gift or complemented us in some way. These are the little social nuances that I am speaking about.

These social conversational nuances can cause us to feel sorry, angry, happy, grateful, successful, upset. We can get mad or cry. These are the things that make us act or react to some-thing said or done. These can be good or bad things. We can perceive them in many different ways. Sometimes the things we say can hurt someone. Sometimes the things we say will make someone happy and feel loved. This includes everything in be-tween. If something we said hurt someone, we might feel bad. If something we said made someone happy, we might feel happy. We use words of gratitude, happiness, love, romance, anger and sadness. These things can be said if we are already angry or happy. If we are sad or grateful. They can show up when we are stressed out or perfectly calm. The phrases we use can be: "I'm Sorry", "Thank You", "I need to apologize for what I said", "I am grateful for what you have done for me", etc. Most people use these phrases a lot. They do not think of them or have any further thoughts about them. They are just a part of life that everyone accepts. People say these things to people without any further thought or explanation. They do not think about it after they have said it. They do not think about it for another minute, hour or entire day. They are little things that are not that im-portant. The bottom line is that if you hurt someone, then you apologize and simply move on. If you are grateful and thank someone for something, then you do so and just simply move on. If anything at all happens, then you deal with it and just sim-ply move on. The key being that you just move on. The average person just uses the phrase that they need and they are done. They just move on with their lives. They do not think about it for minutes, hours or days. They do not wonder if the other person is still upset or still happy. The other person does not even think about it after the issue is resolved. The person who was hurt does not think about it once the apology is issued. The grateful person does not think about the issue once the "Thank You" was heard. All the people involved just move on and don't think about it for one second.

Someone with Obsessive Compulsive Disorder does not necessarily have that option. Thoughts can occur that make you feel that you needed to say "I'm Sorry" or "Thank You" when in fact they were not needed. Sometimes I will obsess over something for hours, days or even a week. I will think about the incident for hours. I will harp on it and it will consume me. I will think about it until I say the key phrase of "I'm Sorry" or "Thank You". It will remain in my brain until these magical words are uttered. Then, I will think about it more and more. Then the repeating and compulsions begin. The numbers begin and the thought lingers. It will go on and on for hours and days. This happens for many different reasons. Many different ideas. Many different thoughts.

There is a part of OCD that no one really mentions. We all know about the checking, repeating, compulsions, thoughts and overall anxiety. There is another type of oddity that is in the OCD package. These are the less discussed OCD feelings. They are included in the OCD lifestyle. They are things that most people with OCD go through, but never really discuss. They are the little weird things that happen to each of us without really being diagnosed as OCD. They must be affected by the same part of the brain that included the OCD. I like to call them OCD's little oddities. They are the things that each of us might go through but rarely mention to a behavior therapist or a doctor of any kind. They are the little weird things that we might go through in a day without acknowledging that they are attached or part of the OCD lifestyle. Either way, they are OCD oddities. Let's explore some of these simple OCD oddities.

"I'm Sorry!" We have all heard this at one point or another. I am sure that most people have used this phrase at some point in their life. Maybe it has been used on more than one occasion. This phrase is actually very common. People use it each and every day. It is used in offices, restaurants, homes, cars, trains, planes, inside and outside. It is used between friends, co-workers, family members, neighbors, in relationships and even between perfect strangers. The truth is that there are many different situations where this phrase can be used. Most people use it as a traditional apology. These apologies are designed to make whomever is involved, feel better. The person who issues the apology feels better that they corrected a mistake that was made. The person receiving the apology feels better that the person acknowledges and had the decency to try and correct the mistake. It is an easy and simple way to remedy a situation where a mistake was made. After the apology is made, hopefully both parties can forget the mistake ever happened and everyone involved can move on. It sounds very dramatic, but is actually very easy.

Apologies are used for a variety of reasons. They are used to correct some sort of error. These errors might be small and insignificant or large and personal. As you can guess, the size of the apology and what is involved will be predetermined by the size of the mistake or error. If you call someone by the wrong name, the apology is a quick and easy "Oh, Sorry!" and that's it. If you break an expensive family heirloom...well...its going to take a lot more than that.

People use the apologies for many different reasons. If you made a mistake at work or home, an apology is needed. If you made a mistake with a close family member or a complete stranger, you will need to apologize. Other mistakes might be an error at work, stepping in front of someone in a line, damaging property, insulting someone, arriving late or not at all to an event, forgetting someone's birthday, getting mad at someone, getting frustrated with a situation, fighting with someone, saying something inappropriate, being mean or rude, making someone feel bad, etc. All of these and more are reasons that an apology is issued. The important thing to realize is that, no matter the reason, each person involved will know when they need to issue an apology. Let's face it, we have all done it. We have issued apologies as well as received them. Hey, it happens, right?

This is not the case with Obsessive Compulsive Disorder. People with OCD have a lot to deal with. One of the symptoms is the famous OCD apology. The OCD apology is one of the many symptoms that are coupled and grouped into the entire OCD package. People with Obsessive Compulsive Disorder tend to apologize a lot. It is a definite symptom. I am not sure if it is due to low serotonin or just plain low self-esteem. I don't know. Either way, people with OCD get to apologize for tons and tons of things. Some days, you can just walk around apologizing for each and everything that you do. This symptom can be very annoying. The major problem with this symptom is that about ninety-nine percent of the time, you do not even need to apologize for something that happened. There is usually no apology even needed or warranted. But still, we apologize.

There are two ways that this happens. One, there is no apology needed but I do it because I feel I should. Two, there is an apology needed and I apologize more than I ever need to. I probably drive the person involved to complete insanity. What makes it even worse is that it all started with a little nothing that the person I am with is not even aware of. The person that I am apologizing to did not even notice something happened. They don't know what I am apologizing for. They often, actually most of the time, tell me that I do not even need to apologize. And still, I repeat that "I'm sorry!".

Later, the OCD apology attaches itself to numbers, sets and places for absolutely nothing. The feeling or reason for the apology is that I feel that I have offended or hurt someone by my actions. This is never true but still, it happens. The fact is that I do not want to hurt anyone's feelings or be an asshole. The OCD blows it up to be a huge catastrophe. I feel as if I picked up an expensive vase and threw it across the room. I feel as if I smashed up their entire house. I feel as if I did something majorly damaging and unacceptable.

My first example of this is when I was talking with a friend about their apartment. They told me that they might want to move and I told them that they should, due to several real problems that I pointed out. I immediately felt as if I need to apologize because I told them that I did not like their current place. I felt bad so I apologized.

Here is another pathetic example. I was talking to another friend and they told me that they wanted to go shopping. I was starved so I told them that we better eat first. They asked "Where?". I said I liked the pizza place. They suggested a sushi bar. I said that I just did not feel like sushi. I felt that my words came out rude. I immediately felt like I needed to apologize for my comments.

Another example is a friend of mine got a new pair of glasses and asked me if I liked them. I told her that they were okay. I immediately felt rude. I then felt that I needed to apologize a few times for my comment. I did. She even said that it was no big deal. But, still the thought and feeling to apologize was there.

I was driving with a friend. She made a turn and went into the wrong lane. I said that she turned into the wrong lane and that she needed to correct it because we were on the wrong side of the street for the next turn we needed to make. I immediately felt as if I was rude and came across angry. I felt that I needed to apologize.

I ate dinner with my family. After we ate, I suggested that I would do the dishes since they cooked. My sister offered to help me. I put a dirty dish on top of the clean dishes by mistake. She told me what I had done and I immediately felt as if I needed to apologize for my actions. I felt that I needed to apologize more than once. The truth is that it was a little nothing and my sister did not even think of it again.

Thank You! People use this phrase all the time. It is usually used as a form of gratitude. People use it if you did something nice for them or helped them in some way. It is used as often as the phrase "I'm Sorry". People use it with friends, family, co-workers and many other people.

I have OCD so I tend to repeat it to people that did something nice for me. I will repeatedly thank them for their actions no matter how small and insignificant their actions were.

I will give you an example of the repeating around a "Thank You". I went on vacation and I asked my neighbor to get my mail while I was away. When I returned, I went to my neighbor's house in order to get my mail. After she handed me my mail, I thanked her. I immediately felt as if I did not say anything. I then felt that I did not thank her. This would mean that I did not show how grateful I was to have her help me. Then, I thought that she would think that I was ungrateful and rude. This is all due to the fact that she did me a favor and I did not thank her. This led to my repeating thank you two more times.

Another example is when I was with my sister. She cooked dinner for me. At the end of the night, I was getting ready to leave. I simply thanked her for dinner. I immediately felt that I did not thank her at all. This would make me rude. I would seem rude because she took the time and made the effort to plan, cook and invite me for dinner. I then had the feeling that I was just leaving without showing my gratitude. I was just eating and walking out. It is hard to deal with. I felt that it would have been rude to just leave. I knew that I thanked her. I heard her say "You're welcome", but still, I felt as if I did not say anything. I then thanked her two more times.

My final example is my birthday. I went to my family's house for a birthday celebration. We ate dinner and had dessert. It was then time for presents. We were all sitting on the couch. There were a few envelopes on the table. I was given the first envelope to open. It was a gift certificate. I said "Thank You". As per usual, I immediately felt that I did not say anything at all. I felt as if I just opened the gift, took it and did not thank the person who gave it to me. I felt as if I just took the gift and sat there silently. I felt as if the person would think that I am rude and ungrateful. I felt that I needed to repeatedly say thank you. Even though, I knew that I already did. I know I said it. I heard them respond to it with a "You're Welcome", but still, I felt as If I said nothing. I just sat there feeling rude. I know that I thanked them, but the thought persisted and lingered for a little while. I then began to repeat. I was in a crowd of people and did not want to show my OCD so I rephrased the thank you a few different ways. All sentences included the word thank you. "Thank you for the gift", "I already know what I will use it for, so thank you", "I can't wait to be able to use it, so thank you". Finally, the repeating was done. I did it enough to know that I actually said it. I was not feeling rude and I completed the numbers. I was finally past this thought and uncomfortable feeling that I was ungrateful. I expressed my thank you and my happiness for my birthday gift. I was done for now.

The bottom line is that the OCD makes everything overblown. Whether it is an apology, a thank you or other feeling. The OCD will take it and run with it. We spend hours and hours on something that just requires a quick and little response. It is unfortunate and creates anxiety and the thoughts/obsessions linger and linger. Anyway, I am sorry that you had to read this chapter. See what I mean?

CHAPTER 9: FORCE OF HABIT!

"Time To Unwind The Mind!"

I would like to revisit "Force of Habit". We have all heard this phrase. There are things that we do as humans on another level. I am sure that the medical profession would describe it as a subconscious impulse. A trained psychiatrist would probably say that these impulses are a second nature way of living. A spiritual advisor would probably say that there is a part of yourself acting on another level and creating this behavior. The bottom line is that I don't know about any of this. I am not a doctor, psychiatrist or spiritual advisor. I'm just a guy that knows that there is such a thing as a force of habit. These habits can be good or bad. We have all heard the terms good habits and bad habits. We have also used the phrase "Get into the habit of..." to describe a training mechanism. This training mechanism is to help you teach yourself to react a different way than you usually do. It is something that you start to do a certain way each time in order to train yourself to perform the task the same way every time in the future. You can also teach yourself to react a certain way to things in your life. The bottom line is that human nature can be trained and taught. These teachings can create a force of habit.

There are good habits such as things that help you or increase your life in a positive way. These repetitive patterns can be training yourself to do a good thing such as always doing the dishes or keeping your home nice and clean. These good habits can be a great way to succeed. They can form a positive force of habit. Maybe a student can use this training to be able to develop good study habits. You can teach yourself good cooking habits. Maybe start a habit of paying your bills the day that you receive them. Maybe you always try to pay your rent or mortgage on time. A child may learn to prepare their clothes for the next day. There are other habits such as brushing one's teeth, taking a shower or going to bed at a decent hour. These are all small examples of good habits.

There are also bad habits. These are habits that we all do with negative results. We continue to perform these habits even with the negative results that we receive. We all know which habits are the bad ones. These are usually the habits that consist of negative actions. These actions can damage one's friendships, family relationships or even damage their own life. They can be behaviors such as smoking, drinking, eating fatty foods, gambling or doing illegal substances. They can also consist of behaviors such as not cleaning your home, your car, your clothes, etc. These are habits that we know to be bad for us, and yet, we still repeat them. We tell ourselves that they are not a problem or that we can stop immediately if we wanted to. The truth is that these negative behaviors are so ingrained in us that they become a strong part of us. These habits turn from a simple indulgence into a major necessity. So much so that we actually lie to ourselves about how bad they actually are. We use the term that "It is no big deal" when in reality, they are VERY big deals. We know for a fact that they are bad for us and that there will, one day, be consequences for our own behavior. The truth is that these negative behaviors are our own fault. Our own manifestation. They might be created to cover up a bigger issue or some unfulfilled part of our soul. It might be that we are hiding the real truth behind these negative behaviors. We cover the real issues with these types of behaviors. They can be excessive in nature. These are all examples of types of negative habits.

The Obsessive Compulsive Disorder has its own force of habit. This is the overwhelming feeling to comply with the rules and regulations that the OCD has. I have described this in a prior chapter as it falls under the OCD umbrella and is not connected to positive and negative behaviors in people in general. I am going to use one example to help explain all of this.

My example will be an alcoholic who is trying to get sober. Drinking excessively to the point of not functioning is obviously a negative behavior and has created a "force of habit". The alcoholic is always thinking about a drink and then starts drinking to relieve the anxiety of being sober for a reason I do not personally understand as I drink alcohol in moderation. The alcoholic can elect a rehab facility and then a support program and successfully return to a productive life. This behavior is not a force of habit compulsion related to OCD but an addiction. The similarity to OCD is the behavior that relieves anxiety.

OCD is a defect in the DNA that I inherited. I learned this when I was eleven years old. Almost forty years later, I am still trying to understand the dynamics of this disease. For purposes of this chapter, I will simply hope that the "force of habit" I have explained previously under the OCD umbrella helps with understanding that it is a separate animal from the positive and negative behaviors in the population at large.

CHAPTER 10: HIDING!

"If The Symptoms Don't Show,
Then Nobody Will Know!"

L et me explain another piece of the OCD puzzle. Hiding the OCD! A lot of articles and doctors don't mention this emotional aspect. There is a lot involved in having to hide the fact that one has OCD. I am an expert at hiding the OCD. There are many things that people can do in order to disguise the symptoms. The entire hiding premise develops at a very young age. For me, it was when my Mother called me in from playing outside with my friends. I was doing some sort of light shaking from Tourette's syndrome. This is a great add on pack to the OCD. Anyway, my Mother told me to try not to shake in public but try to save it for later which is possible with Tourette's Syndrome. I thought that maybe my friends were thinking that it looked weird. Basically, I just learned that this public display of T.S. is not okay. I needed to hide it.

Needless to say, as I got older, the OCD took over as it is apparently the umbrella disease. It became the major issue that needed to be hidden. As the years went on, I understood that my OCD symptoms annoyed others. So, I did not want them to know that I was doing something.   I was around twenty-three years old when I went to behavior therapy as a hopeful treatment. (If you read that chapter, you will know that it was not successful for me.) Anyway, after that, I felt that I should be able to use the behavior therapy to control the symptoms. This made it even more unacceptable to exhibit any further OCD symptoms. Thus, the hiding began. It helped me avoid the biggest taboo: actually telling someone that I had Obsessive Compulsive Disorder. It is a disorder that affects millions and millions of people worldwide. For something so big, it certainly seems like a pretty big secret. It has to be hidden. This is a big emotional hurdle.

I am an expert on hiding my OCD. Over the years, you realize how easy it is to hide the symptoms. The thing that makes it so easy is that most people do not even notice anything. The little ways that I cover my tracks, are a learned skill and if someone sees anything, they will not even think it is odd. The hiding techniques are very tiny and take no time at all. It does take some creativity at times. Once I got used to it, it was smooth sailing from then on. This chapter is not intended to show people how to hide the symptoms. Some people are okay with doing their rituals out in the open. For some reason I am not. So this chapter will show how I hide the symptoms. Let me give you some examples.

The repeating can be difficult to hide as most people will tend to notice that you keep bringing up the same subject matter more than one time. The best way that I cover it up is to just re-word the sentence. It is a quick and painless way to just do the repeating. Most people would not even notice when this happens. If someone you were talking to said "How is the weather?", you would follow it up with "The weather is warm". Then add "You should go outside since the weather is so nice." I like the weather this time of year." Would you even notice? Most people would not even notice that the word "weather" was used three times. This is due to the re-wording. It might feel big to me, especially when I have the anxiety. This will all be internal. No one else even thinks of this type of stuff.

The counting is a different type of symptom. Let's say that you feel like you need to touch a refrigerator three times: I open the refrigerator once and take out a bottle of water. If someone is standing there. I may tell them that I am thirsty but do not want water. Then open the refrigerator door and put the water back. I touched the refrigerator door twice by taking out the water and then putting it back. I will tell them that I changed my mind and will drink the water. Guess what? Did you see it? I opened the refrigerator three times. I got the compulsion done by drinking the water. I guarantee that the person that I am with did not even notice anything. To them, I am thirsty but do not know what I want to drink. This is all it took. I completed the compulsion under the radar. See how easy it is?

Let's say that I want to talk in numbers. I will simply just say three or five things. I am counting. The symptom is repeating. The person that I am talking to does not even know that I am doing it. Here is the example: "Have you seen this movie?". "It is pretty funny." "We do not have to watch it if you do not want to." There, I just said something three times in a perfectly normal way. Most people just call that talking. I am really telling you something with three or five sentences. Most people just think I am having a conversation like every other human. Pretty tricky, right?

I can go out with friends and check the front door. It is not as easy as people will pick up on the fact that I am locking my front door more than once. This is easier than you think as I will make an excuse for my actions that no one will even think twice about. I may walk out with my friends. We all go outside of my house. They are waiting while I lock the door. I stick the key in and lock the front door. I quickly stick the key in again and re-lock the door. I then do it immediately again. Then I shake the handle three times. No one will notice anything. If someone asks or give me an odd look. I simply tell them that "Earlier that day, the door lock felt weird and the handle felt loose." I will add that "I hope I do not need a new door lock or handle." They might make a comment on when that happened to their front door. They might tell me that replacing the front door lock will be easy. They might even offer to help me with it. I will tell them that maybe I will. The reality is that I just got the repeating done and over. I checked my door the OCD number of times and sets. I was with a group of people in a social situation that saw everything. They saw the entire OCD process. They witnessed the thought all the way through the compulsion. I did what I needed to do. I covered it up with two sentences and a normal excuse as to the weird behavior. No one noticed a thing. I am in the clear. I can continue my fun night out with my friends. Most important, they still do not know that I have OCD. Not bad, huh?

Let's say that I need to check the bathroom faucet. There are a few different ways to do this. I can go into the bathroom and pretend to look in the mirror while secretly counting. Sometimes I look rapidly with my eyes from the faucet to the mirror. This can be done quickly and the right number of times. There is another way to do this. Go into the bathroom and physically check the faucet to make sure it is off. If someone catches me, I just tell them that I thought it was dripping. They will not even notice and I got the compulsions done.

Let's say that I am in a friend's house. The OCD is high today. This means that it might trigger anytime and anyplace. I walk by the kitchen table and slightly touch the table top. Since it is a bad day, I instantly feel like I need to check the table top a certain number of times. Okay, this one is a no brainer. When I are talking to my friend, I simply touch the table top and ask what it is made of. I am sure she will tell me the story of the table. Then, I touch it one more time and tell her that the table is very sturdy. I am sure she will agree and tell me how well it is made. Then, I just move the conversation onward. See, no problem.

Let's say I go shopping and pay with a credit card. I take out the credit card in front of the cashier. I swipe it, pay and then put the credit card back into my pocket. If you simply take the credit card back out three times, it will look weird. So, since you already paid, that is once. You take it back out and look at it and put it back into your pocket. Just tell the cashier that you wanted to make sure that you used the right card. Then you do it a third time. This time you tell the cashier that you wanted to check the expiration date as you did not get your new one in the mail yet.

At most, you will get a comment on the banking system from the cashier. Either way, you did the compulsion and nobody even noticed a thing.

I have days where I feel that I need to text someone a certain number of times. The OCD adapts to technology. So, I send a friend three or five one sentence texts. It is common and most people will not notice. Just as a frame of reference "L.O.L." counts as one separate text. You see how easy it is to hide. Most people would get three different lines of text and not question it. I am sure that I am not the only one that does this.

I have a number pop up with an email. Now, as mentioned before, a text is like a live conversation so it is easier to cover up the number compulsions with a certain number of one line texts. An email is not the same. Someone will notice if they get three separate emails with one single line in them. This is more noticeable if you are sending out a work or business email. This can be handled in another number compliant way. Just send an email with three or five separate sentences. I am sure that whatever you are sending or whatever the information that you need get across can easily be split in to a certain number of sentences. Don't forget, "Have a great day." and "Talk to you soon." count as a separate sentence. Pretty easy to do, right.

If I am on a date or with friends in a restaurant where I am paying, I may get the check and need to make sure that I left a good amount for the tip. This is a little more noticeable so it takes some small excuses. I open the bill book and look at it. I quickly calculate the tip. Then leave the tip. Then I open the bill book another time and give an excuse that the receipt is weird the way it is set up. I then close it and quickly open it again. This time my comment is that the font they use is hard to read. Then close it again and I am ready to move one. My date or the friends that I am with do not even notice a single thing. No one has ever questioned it. They still do not know that I did anything odd. Nothing to worry about.

I sometimes get out of my car and feel like I need to check to make sure the trunk is closed. Maybe I need to check the license plate to make sure I brought the right car home. Now, let's say I am with a friend. I need to conceal the reason that I look back. So, I look back once which is normal. I look back a second time saying that my tire looks like it needs air and that I should check it. I then look back a third time. My excuse for the third time is that it looked like my head lights were still on. My friend did not even notice a thing. I got my repeated checking done. They don't know that I am only looking at my car trunk and not anything else.

There are no rules to the OCD. There is really no way to know or one hundred percent predict when a thought will occur. The repeating is pretty standard. With the right experience, you will know when and where it will occur. This is why you need to have a bunch of tricks up your sleeve to cover it up while in public. Let's say that I am outside in a mall or a store. Maybe I am just making a usual trip outside to complete the repeating compulsion. I do not want anybody to notice that I am doing anything. I will simply pretend to scratch my upper lip. This will cover the fact that I am walking somewhere while repeating. People will not see you talking to yourself. They will see a man scratching. This is more normal that saying the same thing over and over again. The subtle scratching is a great way to hide verbal repeating in a public area.

The other component to the repeating is the counting. This is when I count on my hands how many times I am repeating so that I reach the correct number. This can be done by simply putting my hand inside a pants pocket or against my jeans. It can also be done by putting my hand inside of a jacket pocket. People will just see someone walking with a jacket. They will have no idea that I am subtly counting to myself with repeating. It will be no big deal.

Let's say I am at a dinner party. And yes, I may need to EAT in numbers. The OCD starts up and I feel that I need to drink a certain number of glasses of wine. This can be done in two separate ways. The first way is to simply drink five tiny glasses of wine. The glasses would be so small that there is barely anything in each glass. All five glasses would equal one or two normal glasses. Another way would be to pour the wine into my glass in numbers. So, I drip the "Right" number of times into a glass. All of the drips would equal one glass. I can do this multiple times if I feel the need to drink in sets. I can also drink in numbers and sets with any type of beverage. This can be done by taking very small sips. This way, a full beverage will last for me to complete each number and set. Most people at a dinner table would not even notice this. I will just look like I am sitting and drinking at a dinner table. No different than anyone else.

Eventually, dinner will be served. This means that it is now time to eat in numbers. The way that this works is pretty much the same as everything else done a certain number of times. Let's say that I am at a buffet style dinner party. I will line up and grab a plate. While moving past the food, I simply will begin to count everything on my plate. This is done in terms of servings or amounts of everything you put on your plate. An example would be a piece of chicken, a scoop of rice and a vegetable. To everyone else, this is a normal plate of food. Everyone will talk in line and no one will even notice. To the person with OCD, there are three items on the plate. You see what I mean by, eating in numbers?

If I am at a breakfast buffet, it is just as easy to do this in numbers and sets. Let's say it is a horrible day and the OCD, for whatever reason, has skyrocketed. The numbers and sets will be very strong and adamant. So, it is time to eat a nice breakfast in a meaningless stream of numbers. So, I am in line and moving across the huge restaurant buffet of food. I can serve three tiny spoons of scrambled eggs. Then an English muffin and some bacon. I know what you are thinking, this should raise the number too much. An English muffin is two pieces and the bacon is a few strips. I get it, but for some reason, these can count for "items" on the plate. Believe me, I don't get it either. The eggs are one item. The English muffin is two separate pieces, but count as one item. The bacon counts as one item. This is three things on the plate. I may add one link of sausage for a fourth item. Then a pastry as five items. Now, if the numbers are so high that the sets are involved, I will need to go back to the buffet for another set of five. This is easier if I am hungry. I can then go back and get three pastries, a small scoop of eggs and a small scoop of potatoes. There is my second set of five items. Everybody makes multiple trips with little portions to try everything. It is perfectly normal and no one without OCD will even notice. They don't count so they just see a normal person trying everything just like everyone else there. Congratulations! You just learned to eat your first meal in numbers. Yup! Welcome to my world.

The prior paragraphs are about dealing with the numbers in public. This may actually happen at home too. I might feel the need to eat in numbers and have three different things while cooking. This can also be done by simply adding three toppings or spices to something you are cooking. Maybe three types of snacks. Pretzels, almonds and chips all add up to three in my book. You see how it works.

By now you know how difficult the OCD can be. People with OCD might be much more comfortable staying home. Most people think we all have social anxiety. No! We might just feel better staying at home. To someone with OCD, a person's home is a safe zone. It is a relaxed place. The first reason is that everything inside is yours, and I am sure, OCD free. The second reason is that you are in control of the elements. There is no worry that the OCD will be triggered by accident. There is no fear of social incidents that might occur. No OCD to hide from such as conversations. There is nothing to avoid. There is no dirt or cleanliness issues to wash repeatedly. No car doors to check. No wallet to check. If you drop your wallet or credit card, it is inside your own house where it is safe. No outside interference what so ever.

No job issues. No outside stress. It is plain and simple, a more relaxed place. One of the great things about being at home is the antithesis of this chapter: No OCD to have to hide! This is, of course if you live alone and I do.

If I am living with someone, it can be a parent, friend or significant other. This, of course, makes the hiding much more difficult. This is especially true if the person I live with knows what to look for in terms of compulsions. If they know the system. If they know what I might be doing. I have lived with many people over the years. Here are some of the ways that I have concealed the OCD symptoms.

Let's start off by talking in numbers and sets. As you know, the numbers are when I say something a certain number of times. The sets are when I use the same subject matter in a certain number of places. This can become tricky. You will need to enlist some creativity.

Let's say I am sitting on the couch with whomever I live with. I feel that I need to discuss something in three sets. For this example, I will use a movie as the subject matter. I will say three or five sentences regarding the movie. Those sentences would all equal one complete set. The person I am with, will reply. The replies do not matter for these examples so let me focus on the OCD instead. So, I have done one complete set of the movie repeating. I can simply get up and walk into the kitchen. The couch is one place and the kitchen is another. So, I have completed the first set by leaving the couch. Now, I am in the kitchen. I can simply grab some water and bring it back to the couch. I then discuss the movie in numbers again. This is set number two. The person I am with will respond. I have now completed set number two. I can get up again and go into the kitchen, then get a napkin and bring it back to the couch and place it under my water. Then, say a few more things about the movie. The person will simply respond. Now, I can get up and go to the bathroom. I have just completed a set of three. I have spoken about the movie three times and in three separate sets. The person I am with will not even notice. To them, it was one long conversation where I got some water, realized I needed a napkin and then went to the restroom. That is all. They do not think in numbers like someone with OCD so it will not even register that you were doing compulsions.

Let's say the compulsion is to repeat something in a certain number of sets. These sets require a different place for each set. So, I will need to figure out a way to do this without the person I am living with seeing the OCD. This can be done in many different ways. The best way is the garbage. If I feel to repeat about, hmmm, I'll use the car door being locked. Just an example: If I need to repeat that the car door is locked in five separate places. Then, I can do it with the garbage. By the way, this method also works for any type of repeating. It can be a subject matter, an event coming up, something from work, an errand or even a vacation. Here is how this works. I will use both the repeating in numbers and in sets.

I am in my house like every normal day. I think and say in my head: "The car door is locked." I then feel that I need to repeat it. Now that I have started the numbers, I will need to complete the compulsion. Since one of my numbers is five and I have already said it twice in my head, I say three "The car door is locked.", "The car door is locked.", "The car door is locked." All this in my head. That is one set inside my house. With the correct experience, I know what needs to be done. I simply go into the kitchen, reach under the sink and grab the bag of garbage. I mention to the person I am with, that I am going to throw the garbage. A normal thing, right? I go outside with the garbage. I am now outside of the house which makes it a different location and therefore a different set. I calmly mumble, "The car door is locked." "The car door is locked." "The car door is locked." "The car door is locked." "The car door is locked.". I throw the garbage and go back into the house. The house is a different location so that I am cleared for another set. I am in the bathroom washing my hands. Since I live with someone, I say again in my head. "The car door is locked." "The car door is locked." "The car door is locked." "The car door is locked." "The car door is locked.". That completes set number three. Now, I have two left. One small detail. There is no more garbage. So, it is time for a new excuse to go outside for more fun and enjoyable repeating. Now what? Aha! Most people have old delivery boxes that they put aside or packaging from an order that they have not thrown out yet. Now, here comes the creativity. I threw the only garbage. Yep, you guessed it! I find one of the packages that I intended to throw out at some point in time. I grab it and start to walk out. I make the excuse to whomever I live with that I keep forgetting to throw this package out. I go outside and let it rip. "The car door is locked." "The car door is locked." "The car door is locked." "The car door is locked." "The car door is locked.". That is four sets. You come into the house. You wash your hands in the bathroom. Time for set number five. You are back inside so you silently repeat to yourself. "The car door is locked." "The car door is locked." "The car door is locked." "The car door is locked." "The car door is locked.". Now all five numbers and sets are accounted for. Plus, you also took care of some chores along the way. You threw the nightly garbage as well as cleaned out the packaging that you have been "meaning" to throw out. Pretty good, right. Wrong! There is one tiny problem. I repeated the fifth set in the house. I am still in the house. If you read the rule book of the laws of Obsessive Compulsive Disorder, you will see in section A, paragraph 4, roman numeral 2.... Alright, I am kidding. The point is that with OCD. I must COMPLETE all sets. If I stay in the house, I am still in set five since the repeating was done there. Since, it is a nice summer night, I just tell whoever I live with that I feel like sitting outside. Assuming I have a place to sit outside. If not, I can go for a walk. Maybe I can just check the mailbox to see if there is any mail. The point being is that I need to go outside one more time in order to complete the fifth set. Once I do that, I am done. The repeating is done. The numbers and sets are all present and accounted for. The compulsions are completed. Now, to the person with OCD, it is just a normal day filled with mind numbing worthless compulsions. To the person without OCD, they just saw someone throw the nightly garbage, realize they forgot another piece of garbage and threw it out, then went outside to relax on the patio. See what I mean? I did the entire compulsion. I hid the entire pro-cess thus hiding/covering up the OCD completely. Pretty easy, right?

If I am in a place in public that needs to count as a compulsion location, I can use a few different tricks. I can check my phone or just look at my watch. Most people will just think that I am just walking slowly because I am checking a text, or to see if I missed a call or to see what time it is. No one will notice that I am actually repeating to myself in numbers.

Sometimes the OCD hits while I am shopping. I may look at a product a certain number of times for reassurance. Clothing is a great example of this. If I am shopping for shirts, I can check to make sure that the size is correct or read the washing instructions. If the OCD hits, I just grab the label or tag and do my visual counting compulsion. A visual counting compulsion can be completed in two separate ways. One, I can look or stare at the label while counting. Two, I can rapidly move my eyes from the label to the floor and back. This is done extremely rapidly. Each time I look back at the label will constitute as one. If the number is three, just do it three times. If someone thinks it's odd or asks me what I am looking at, I just tell them that I was reading to see what it is made of and what the washing instructions are. It will seem perfectly normal. The visual compulsions are much easier to hide. The reason being is that, as you read my examples, you can see that I can present different forms of excuses. The reason it is easy to hide is that no one really sees or knows what I am ac-tually looking directly at. It is also a less physically obvious form of compulsion.

Let's say I am on the street while walking with a friend. Sometimes I feel that I need to re-tie my shoes a couple of times. I can bend down and re-tie one shoe. The best way is to count while yanking the laces a few times. Most people will not even notice. If someone does, I just tell them that I have to make sure the laces are tight. I tell them that they loosen easily. I will add that I hate these laces as they always untie. It is no big deal.

Let's say I need to do some repeating in a certain number of places while someone is home or friends are over. Instead of doing a large compulsion in front of people that will take time: Remember the garbage throwing compulsion? It might spark questions. I can simply stand in the doorway with one foot in the house and one foot outside. I pretend that I heard something. The inside will count as one place and the outside will count as another. I can perform the compulsion by switching my weight from one foot to the other. Each time I lean on a foot, it will count as being in that place. If I do the repeating while leaning back and forth, it will count as if I physically walked in and out of the door. It is a lot less conspicuous. It can be done very quick and fast. I can do this multiple times in order to complete the compulsion. If I do it one time, that will be one set. Then, I just do as many sets as needed. I can just tell someone that I am checking the weather outside to see if it is nice. I can do this same compulsion in different places such as my car: Open the front door and lean in with one foot inside and one foot outside. I can do the same leaning on both sides of the car. I can then do all the repeating. No one will notice this. They will just think that I am thinking of something or forgot something. I can check my watch or phone while doing this. The reality is that I can do this is in a certain number of places. This will cover me on the number of sets I need to do. I can also accomplish this by just calmly tapping your toe. No one will see that anything is wrong.

Let's say it is a sunny day and I am on my patio. I suddenly feel that I need to walk in and out of my house a certain number of times. I am within the vision of my neighbors who are able to see me physically walking in and out of the house several times. OK, get this! I go into my house and pour a small drink of water and go back outside. Then, after finishing the water, I can go back inside the house and come back with another glass of water. My neighbors will just think that I am thirsty and I am simply going inside the house to replenish the drink. This can also be done with other items. I can then go in and come out with a snack. Then, I can go in and come back out with a phone or iPad. If someone does notice, they will just think that I am snacking on a hot day. They will have no idea that I am doing OCD compulsions. They, without OCD, will not count how many times I came in and out. Only I will know the numbers that I am following. I will be the only one who knows that I seem to be relaxing on a hot summer day but I actually walked in and out of my house three or five times.

If I drive to go shopping with my friends, I may need to put stuff in the trunk of the car. I may feel that I need to slam the trunk a certain number of times. The obsession might be that the trunk is not locked if you do not close it a certain number of times. If this happens, I simply close the trunk, open it and re-close it a few times. I can add a puzzled look on my face in order to sell it. I can just tell my friends that it has not been latching properly. Simply move on and so will they.

I have had to use the car as a separate place for repeating. This is a good place as I am alone and can freely repeat in whatever numbers are needed. The easiest way
is to have a few excuses as to why I need to go to my car. I do not need to drive somewhere. It might be late at night or there are no errands that need to be completed. This can be solved by telling whoever I live with that I need to check to make sure that I locked my car. Or maybe I think I left something in it. Then, I run out and get into the car. I do all the repeating needed. Then, simply return to the house. No problem.

I have started this chapter with some of the ways that the OCD can be hidden in my personal life. It can be hidden in my home, stores, cars and even your friend's homes. But what about all of our professional lives? I am guessing that we all need some hiding there. The OCD does not take time off so that you can do your day job. In the world of OCD, there is no professional courtesy. Like most people, we all need to work for a living. This can be done in many different ways. I have mainly worked in the professional office environment so that is my experience.

This usually raises the OCD due to circumstance. The circumstance being that you do not want to screw something up or make a mistake. This is why the OCD skyrockets. Let's face it, you might have the best boss in the world. You might love the people you work with. You might work in a relaxed and low stress environment with no deadlines whatsoever. Even with that, there are still many things that can go wrong. There are files, invoices, contracts, databases, meetings, proposals, estimates, charts and graphs, clients and their needs and coworkers. All of these things can contribute to the OCD. An office is where most of the "Screwing Up" or "Mistake" obsessions occur. There might be some simple compulsions or major ones. Either way, the more details your job entails, the more there is to worry about. The OCD will take its toll on everything from checking to make sure that you spelled a client's name correctly in an email to being in charge of a department full of people and everything in between.

Either way, there are many things in an office that can trigger OCD. This creates many different situations where compulsions need to be hidden. It is much more difficult to hide OCD in a professional environment. The reason being that, no matter the level of OCD, you still need to get your job done. Sometimes you will need to get creative. It might take some creative reasons and excuses for the behavior. Let's explore some of the examples of this type of compulsion hiding.

Let's say that you are in a cubicle or some other place where you are in plain view of your co-workers. You are sending a business email. The obsession hits where you feel that you did not spell the client's name correctly. Now, remember you are in a high traffic office. You need to be more careful when doing the compulsions in this setting. So, you can simply open the email, write it and begin the ridiculous compulsions. You can simply stare at the name and re-read it until the number set is complete. If someone sees, just let them know that you are proofing the body of the email to make sure that you have included all of the important information correctly. No one will suspect a thing. The best part of the visual compulsion is that no one sees that you are counting or repeatedly doing something physical. You can even use a prop. Just get an invoice or contract and leave it open on your desk in front of you. You can then point back and forth from your desk to the computer screen. Anyone that happens to walk by will just think that you are double checking the information in the email and matching it up to the terms of the contract or amount on the invoice. It is simple and perfect.

Sometimes you just have anxiety or feel uncomfortable. You may have an itch. The second you scratch it; you feel that you need to do it a certain number of times. While doing it, someone notices. Maybe you are at lunch with your usual lunch crowd or in a close knit meeting. You can simply mention that you have a pain wherever the itch happens to be. Just mention that you are sore from the gym. This is a very normal thing. Everyone, at some point or another, has tweaked a muscle while working out. No one will question it.

You might be walking to a meeting or going to a file room. You and a coworker start a conversation. The OCD dictates that you need to talk about that conversation in a certain number of places. You can do this by continuing the conversation. Simply count out the locations as you keep the conversation going. If the number is a five, simply count out five places. The locations can be the file room, the hallway, the elevator, coffee room and the conference room where the meeting is being held. Your coworker will not even notice as they will not even be counting anything. To them, they are just walking and talking with a coworker or friend. They will see it as just a normal conversation on the way to a corporate meeting or event. Nothing odd or unusual.

Imagine that you have payroll checks that need to be locked in a desk drawer. With OCD, your first thought would be that you do not want this responsibility. The second thought would be the amount of checking that this responsibility will cause. Anyway, you put the checks in a drawer in your desk and lock it. You check to make sure that the drawer is locked securely. Then, the obsession that the drawer is unlocked or can be opened appears. This will start the process of worrying that someone will be able to steal the checks, people will not get paid and you will be responsible for it. The compulsions will make you feel better about locking the drawer. You will need to check the drawer in numbers and sets. You do as many sets as you can without anyone noticing. If someone does notice that you have pulled on the drawer many times, you simply tell the coworker that saw you that the drawer shut weirdly and you are nervous about it. Maybe you can add that the drawer was locked and still opened at one point. The person might not respond. They might even offer up a story about their desk drawer as well. The point being that no one will notice that it was actually OCD.

You might work in a company with a corporate kitchen. There is usually cheap coffee, plastic utensils, paper plates and cups, a soda machine and a fridge. These kitchens are usually where the entire department gets coffee to begin to fuel up for the day of work. As soon as the first employee arrives, they will make a fresh pot of coffee. If you are the first employee to arrive, you will make the coffee. You put the ground coffee into the machine, the coffee pot in place and hit the "Brew" button. You might get an obsession that you did not put the coffee pot in the correct place. This would mean that the pot is off center or crooked. This will lead to the coffee spilling all over the place. It will make a real mess. It will be your fault. So, you will want to stay and continue checking it. The best way to do this is to stand right near it while making sure that it is okay and that coffee is not spilling everywhere. You can just stand there with your cup in hand. To you, you are secretly checking to make sure you did it correctly. You might even use the visual compulsions in order to check the correct number of times. To someone else or a coworker, you are just tired and waiting for the first cup of coffee. If someone else walks into the kitchen. Just tell them that you did not sleep well and you are exhausted. Tell them that you are waiting for caffeine. Your coworker might even laugh. Easy, right?

Imagine that you are in charge of entering a new vendor payment into the company database. This payment is due to the specific vendor's contract details. You go into the file room and grab the contract you need. You might get an obsession where you grabbed the wrong contract. This will result in you entering the incorrect information into the company database. All of this will lead to creating incorrect invoices. The bottom line: you feel that your boss will be upset. This is a mistake that you do not want to make. You will want to make sure that you have the correct contract. Instead of standing there and reading the number over and over while counting on your fingers, just open the contract and pretend to read a memo in the file. In reality, you are holding a memo while actually repeatedly reading the contract number over and over to make sure it is the correct contract. Anyone who sees you will just think that you are reading a memo in a contract. No big deal.

You are now in your boss's office. He or She is telling you how to finish the project you are working on. If it is Friday, your boss may tell you that it can be done on Monday. To confirm, you ask "Are you sure Monday will be enough time?". They will respond and then you can say "Monday it is!". Maybe you add "Monday will work better because I will have the entire day to complete it." They will agree with you. This might have started with an obsession that you did not hear the right day they needed it. They may need it by Friday night. You might need to work on the weekend. Basically, the obsession is that you did not hear it correctly and you will not have the project done in time. As you can see, the repeating was done. It was quick. Your boss will, most likely, not even notice. If they did, it will not be a big deal. They might think it was weird that you acted that way. Overall, it will be a short thought and easily forgotten. Remember, people without OCD will forget about something much easier than someone with OCD. The major takeaway is that you did the repeating and confirmed the actual deadline for the project to be completed.

Like most companies, there are tons of meetings. The first aspect of a meeting is that you do not want to be late for it. With OCD, it is difficult because you are worried about getting ready for the meeting. Now you can add the fact that the OCD will make you feel as if you do not remember the time of the meeting correctly. To handle this, you simple send a coworker an email. You include the time, date and where the meeting is. They will usually confirm that the information is correct. You can reply that you will see them then. The reason is that if the information or time of the meeting is not correct, they will correct it in a reply email. This will end the worry that you have made a mistake. You will also get them to confirm that you have the information correct. Then, if the OCD persists, it will be in your email. Now you will have confirmation and an email that you can keep checking or print out and re-read. This will ensure that you will not be late for any important meetings. This will enable you to satisfy the OCD. To your coworker, you are just confirming a meeting time and date. Your coworker will not even notice anything odd went on. They will not suspect that you have OCD. Simple enough, right?

Do you go to the bathroom at work? Yup, you will need to wash your hands a certain number of times. This can be done easily even if someone is in the room with you. Simply wash once without soap, once with soap, and another time without soap. Most people will not even notice. Another solution is to wash your hands once and wait for the other person or people to leave. This can be done by looking in the mirror and checking your outfit or hair. Everyone does it. No one will even notice that you are doing anything. Then, as soon as they leave, do the washing compulsions quickly and you are done.

The overall repeating is more difficult to hide when you

are in a professional environment. The main reason is that the people in the office are coworkers and bosses. They are not good friends or family that you are relaxed with. It is not as easy to bring up the same subjects or use the same words many times in a sentence or conversation. But it can be done very easily. It just needs some creativity to move it along. There might be sentences that sound like this: "Monday we need to meet before the client comes.". "Monday, right?". "What time do you want to meet on Monday?". To your coworker, you are just trying to re-member when the client is coming. Very normal. I am sure they have done it themselves. To you, you are repeating and doing a compulsion while hiding the OCD completely. The basic point is that you will have tons of repeating to do at work. You will need to repeat in numbers and sets. It will be annoying. It can be done very easily and hidden completely.

Let's finish our work day, shall we? At the end of the day, most people just turn off their computer, grab a few personal items and head home. This might not be the case for someone with OCD. You can turn off your computer. You may feel as if the computer is not logged out from a company database or that your email program is open. The bottom line is that you might have some checking to do. If you stand in your cubicle and stare at the computer while everyone is passing you and saying "Goodnight!" or "See you tomorrow!", it will be noticeable and might look odd. If you continue to go back to your cubicle over and over, it might look weird. There are many different excuses that are easy to explain if needed. You might tell your coworkers that you forgot something at your desk. You might say that you wanted to write a last minute reminder note for something that you have to do first thing in the morning. Maybe you tell them that you thought you saw the phone message light on. You can tell people that you needed to put something away, or leave someone a message. All of these excuses are normal and happen to people every day. The point is that no one will know that you are actually going back to your computer to repeatedly stare at your computer while counting to a certain number or set of numbers. All of this is to try and cover or end a thought that your computer is still on and the company's sensitive information is available to anyone who walks by. These excuses are all very easy ways to cover up any OCD that might arise.

Here are my final thoughts on hiding the OCD because it is basically hiding a major part of myself. It is something that makes me...well...ME! With OCD, I need to constantly pretend that nothing is wrong or that I am simply fine. This is a difficult task because I am hiding who I actually am. I need to hide something that is so big in my life. It takes so much of my time and energy to control. I need to hide the main thing that is in everything I do. I need to hide the obsessions. I feel the need to do the ridiculous compulsions that follow the obsessions. It is laced in almost everything that I do. It is involved in things small and large. It starts the second I do anything from something small like sending an email to something large like taking a vacation to another country. It is there when I cook, clean, walk, talk, look, eat, shop. It is in everything that I do when I am with other people such as work, errands, social events, dinner parties, dates, hang out with friends, travel with family or just watching a game on TV. No matter what I do, the OCD is with me.

Another aspect of this is that I need to hide something that has caused so much emotional pain in my life. I have suffered in silence for many years. It causes pain each and every hour that I am awake. The good days are better because it is low. The bad days leave me to acknowledge that it is bad and uncontrollable. It is a constant stream of pain and suffering. It leaves me angry at times. It leaves me sad at times. Either way, it has totally disrupted my life.

I need to spend just as much time hiding my OCD it as it takes to do it. The fact that I have to "Get Good" at hiding these compulsions is ridiculous. It is horrible to have to make up such stupid excuses for the reason I need to do something. How many times can I "Throw the garbage" or "Check the car"? It is so ridiculous that I have to "Come Up" with excuses for doing these strange things. "Oh, excuse me. I need to go outside to throw out my shoelaces one at a time." How many nights can I come up with an excuse as to why I need to throw the garbage three times in one night? How many times can I try to look normal while throwing out the packaging from a delivery separately. Meaning, I throw out the carton, the inside packaging and the direct packaging all in separate trips. How many ridiculous excuses can I use as to why I need to go out and lock my car? It is either locked or unlocked. Most cars will not need to be locked three to five times. How many times do I have to make an excuse to friends, family and coworkers such as "Something I forgot" and have to go back for? Why does it take me so long to send a simple email? It is hard to have to come up with these stupid reasons as to why I want to sit and relax outside during a lightning storm or take a walk at midnight in my pajamas during a snow storm. I constantly make excuses for the weird or odd behavior. This is all to cover up the ridiculous compulsions that the OCD creates. It gets old having to come up with these pathetic excuses day in and day out. The fact that I even have to do this takes an emotional toll. Coming up with excuses for the odd things or behaviors that someone might notice is hard. The mere idea that I have to use these stupid tricks to cover up the OCD hurts me.

You see how many instances or tasks that the OCD is involved in. You see what it takes to cover it. Now, think of all the situations where they might occur. You need to cover multiple compulsions each and every hour. Sometimes in each and every minute. It is very difficult to know that you need to hide the things you do when other people do not. You are stuck with anxiety and doing odd things. It is not easy to see people that do not have OCD breezing through these little daily things. I know that everyone has it hard in life. I will add that, to someone like me with OCD, it is harder to know that most people in your life do not have to live like this. You spend years watching your family doing the things that I have mentioned in this chapter with ease.

The friends you have that just go through life without having to do these things, think these thoughts or feel these feelings. They do not have to constantly yell at themselves and say that they are not going to do compulsions. They don't need to try different medications every few years. They do not need to go to neurologists every few months. They do not have to listen to people with advice on why they have OCD and how they can get rid of it. They do not have to read articles on how to help themselves. They do not have to listen to people constantly asking them if they are repeating, counting or doing something. They do not have to cry when the OCD can not be controlled. They do not have to feel like they ruined a vacation, dinner party, holiday dinner, birthday party or social event with the OCD. They do not need to fight with themselves. The basic point is that they can simply just live...PERIOD!!! It must be nice. I wish I knew what it felt like.

Hiding the OCD comes with the territory. It is never discussed. It is a sub category of the OCD. It is a part of the OCD. It is just as common as the obsessions. It goes right with the compulsions. While doing one, you are doing the other. It should be called Obsessive Compulsive Hiding Disorder. The easy part of the hiding process is that most people do not even notice that you are doing something. They might, at most, think that you did something weird or odd. If they do not have OCD, they will simply and most likely forget about it. It will be nothing to them. To us with OCD, it is a major issue for days on end. We live in hope that no one will notice these little things that we are doing.

CHAPTER 11: A WAY OF LIFE AND THE EMOTIONS THAT FOLLOW!

"A Ton Of Pain With Absolutely No Gain!"

Let me start out by saying that this chapter is not meant to depress anyone. It is meant to explore the psychological side of OCD. The fact is that we have a lot to deal with as do all people with a handicap. I feel that people with OCD need to acknowledge that there are many emotions that are caused from the struggle of living with this particular disorder. I myself know these emotions all too well. This is why I have chosen to include this discussion. Good! Bad! Indifferent! Either way, these emotions are there.

The difficult life of someone with Obsessive Compulsive Disorder begins at a very young age. Most children discover this under the age of ten. That is when a person begins to notice that their life is hard. You realize that you are, in fact, different than the other children in your family and from the kids you go to school with. I spent a lot of my childhood going to doctors to finally discover that I actually had Obsessive Compulsive Disorder. I was eleven years old and had to learn what it was and what this meant. I always felt that all of what was happening was my fault. My diagnosis freed me from the negative emotions associated with this idea. But at the same time, I now knew that I would not have what was considered a normal life.

As the years go by, you meet with many many doctors. Each doctor has their own theory as to what will work for you. They all ask you what your symptoms are as well as for a demonstration. They all recommend the new medications that are on the market. They all mention the value of the Cognitive Behavior Therapy (CBT). They basically make you listen to their song and dance. You know that they do not have OCD and you wonder if they even know what they are talking about. As they drone on and on, you realize that they cannot really help you.

As you can tell by reading my book, you probably spend most of your life researching and looking for your own solution. The real reason is that there is still the hope that you will stumble upon the solution that will give you the freedom to live a somewhat carefree life. You tend to do online research to see what others are going through with their symptoms. You research the new medications that are out there. As you do, you quickly learn that most of these new medications have horrible side effects. They would actually make things a lot worse. A lot of time can be spend searching through many different resources. The medical resources can be from major universities, famous hospitals and worldwide OCD associations. Most of the research ends up nowhere. It is so depressing. An article might mention something you already know, have tried or looked into at some point. Most of which simply did not work. For every article, there are so many people who try the suggestions and mention that they did not work. For every medication, there are thousands of people who are miserable on their dosage because there is no relief.

The point is that you can read all of the articles, go to all of the doctors and do all of the research. They are all written by high level doctors and researchers with tons and tons of degrees. They mention lists and lists of symptoms. They have lists and lists of medications. They have lists and lists of treatment options. The major thing that is left out of a lot of the articles I have read are the emotions. The true and hard emotional toll that Obsessive Compulsive Disorder takes on a human being that is suffering. It takes a lot out of a person trying to live one full day with OCD. You have a lot of emotions to deal with caused by all the symptoms you have to deal with. It is only logical that something that consumes so much of one's life will take its emotional toll. And the common panacea of an anti-depressant just does not cut it. The medical response is more anti-depressant if there is no relief. Well, NO! It makes you into a zombie.

The emotional toll starts off the day you find out that you officially have Obsessive Compulsive Disorder. It is a tough day. It is worse as most of us find out when we are really young. This changes the life we thought we would have. You don't even know what OCD is or what it entails. Basically, you are very young and just got diagnosed with something that you have never heard of. It is a lot for a young child to deal with. But as you grow, you start to settle into your OCD symptoms. Through dealing with your symptoms, you realize that there are some things that you cannot do. This is usually a minor upset, but it's not not the end of the world.

The major emotional problems began for me when I was twenty-two. This is when the major depression and pain from my OCD started. Ever since then, it has been a struggle to live with. The emotions from living with OCD had taken a big toll on my life. The day in and day out of life with OCD left no room for positive feelings such as satisfaction, contentment, happiness and some joyfulness. On that uplifting note, let me try to explain the trials and tribulations of what someone with OCD goes through in their lifetime.

The hardest aspect of living with OCD for me; is knowing that the entire system is not real. The thoughts are not real. The OCD numbers should not exist. The anxiety is uncontrollable and triggered by this fake system. The medical community refers to these thoughts as irrational obsessions. I have had thousands of these irrational obsessions. They have a fancy name. The reality is that these thoughts are fake. They are pure crap. There is a part of my brain that creates and delivers them to my consciousness. I get thoughts that have no bearing on the real world. Imagine finding out that a big percentage of your daily thoughts are nonsense. How would you feel?

These irrational thoughts come out of nowhere. I am going about my day just like everyone else and boom...there is a thought. It is not planned and certainly not wanted. It can happen anywhere or anytime. Either way, you now have a thought that needs to be dealt with. It is very hard to know that you have to manage a thought that is not real. The thoughts that are so strong, believable and realistic are simply not real. It is a fake thought. I live with the fact that most people only have real thoughts. I have fake thoughts. I can not tell you how many times I have hung out with friends, family and coworkers. All of which are perfectly calm with a clear head. I, on the other hand, have a large fake thought lingering all day. I have to spend most of my life fighting my own brain. Repeatedly telling myself that the thought is not real or that it is just the usual OCD. I have to spend a lot of time talking back to my own brain. Imagine that you are having fun with your friends. Relaxing, eating, drinking, etc. All of a sudden, you get a thought that if you don't have three tiny sips of water, you get Cancer. How would you feel? Would you be able to continue a fun dinner party while remaining relaxed? I didn't think so. Gee that's fun. No psychological damage whatsoever, right?

I live in numbers. I spend my entire life counting to make sure that I do everything in my life the "Right" number of times. This is very hard. It is also depressing. The reality is that I spend too much time doing everything "correctly". My numbers are three and five. The fact is that three and five feel the best for me. I know that the numbers are not real or logical. Let's face it, OCD numbers do not even exist. Yes, numbers exist. There is math, physics, money, percentages, etc. These are the real numbers. I am only talking about the OCD numbers. Obviously, one and one is still two. That is real. If I check my stove five times; is it turned off more or better five times rather than once. No! This is what I mean by the numbers are not real. I live with the numbers. Everything has to be a certain number of times. If not, I get anxiety and a thought. If I wash my hands once with soap. They are clean. If I wash my hands five times. Are they any more clean? Nope! I may make a mistake or yell at someone. If I apologize once. It is done. I apologized for my mistake. Everyone can move on. If I apologize five times; did I apologize better or just more? Does the other person accept it more. Nope! I live with these numbers every single day of my life. I do things in numbers, talk in numbers, repeat tasks in numbers, eat in numbers, look at things in numbers, read in numbers, cook in numbers, etc. I spend my day making everything correct in a system that is pure fantasy. The OCD numbers are just not real. It does not matter how many times you do something. Most people if asked would not know how many drinks they had or how many times they said a word. I would know. This is what makes the OCD so hard to live with. What is that information good for? Can you turn your numbers in for money? If I check my stove five times, will someone pay me five dollars? Plain and simple, living in numbers is a waste of life. It is so frustrating. There is no point to counting everything you do and purposely doing things a certain number of times. The reality is that all people with OCD waste their time and life doing things or focusing on things that are just not real. A true distraction from one's life. The difficult part is that I know this entire system is brain garbage and I still obey it. I still pay attention to it. I still comply with it. It makes me feel weak, not strong. It destroys my self-esteem. My entire life is spent making sure that I listen and behave within a false system of events. It takes a ton of time and effort. It makes me not want to do anything productive. It is physically exhausting. Mentally draining. Most of all, it really sucks the fun and enjoyment out of my life. The little insignificant things that people take for granted are an OCD nightmare for someone like me.

Here is a random example of a stressful situation that someone with OCD will face. I have sat on the couch with my sister and nephews. We are at my sister's home watching a movie. Everyone is relaxed and enjoying the movie. I am not. I am frozen with level 8 anxiety. I am trying to ignore the anxiety and pay attention to the movie. It is not easy watching your entire family completely relaxed and laughing at a movie while I sit there filled to the brim with anxiety. It does not allow me to feel the happiness and contentment that I should feel when I am with the family I love. I need to devote eighty percent of my energy to the OCD and a mere twenty to the movie. I have to sit there with my sister and her kids, pretending that I am happy, relaxed, calm and engrossed in the movie. This type of situation can occur in various ways. The worst part is the idea that I even have to get this anxiety in the first place.

One of the main things with OCD is the issue of avoidance. People with OCD tend to avoid things which they know will cause or trigger the OCD. An example of this is a simple conversation. Maybe the subject matter triggers the OCD. Let's use this as an example: I show up at my Mother's house on a Saturday. We are going to have lunch. I am about to go on a vacation but want to avoid the discussion. I will not mention it. We are in her house getting ready to leave. She simply asks "Are you all packed?" This starts the number compulsions. I respond with a "Pretty Much." The subject matter is the vacation. The compulsion number is five. I need to now talk to her about the vacation five times. Either way, I hope that my Mother does not discuss or even say the word "Vacation"
to me or it will be another set of five for the both of us. My Mother does not have OCD. She does not live in numbers. She has no idea that she is doing the compulsions as if they were her own.

Another form of avoidance is that there are just some subjects that you don't like. They can be childhood memories, old relationships, bad jobs, etc. So, with OCD, you just try to keep away from those conversations. This is not easy as someone might start talking about them. People without OCD have the freedom to discuss any topic they want so they might start a conversation about a bad subject matter. I have been in this situation more than I care to admit. You have a few choices when this occurs.

Talk about it and use behavior therapy. Talk about it and do the number compulsions with the person. You can always repeat to yourself about it in many different ways to fulfill the compulsion numbers. If someone brings up a bad subject matter, then you just sit in complete anxiety until they shut up. I have also ended conversations for the simple reason that the compulsion was completed. This means that I have used up my numbers for this subject so I cannot discuss it anymore. That's a fun one especially when you need to find out important information about something. Either way, it is no picnic.

I tend to live around how the OCD will react to certain things. With experience, I have learned what my triggers are. I am not always as social as I would like to be due to the OCD. It is always easier to stay home and avoid earthly encounters. This is due to the fact that my house is a safe zone. I do not have to hide the OCD. Basically, I tend to let the OCD control my life. People with OCD spend a lot of time living in fear that the OCD will be triggered. With that, comes hours of thoughts and compulsions in order to clean up the mess. It all takes time. With OCD, you tend to live in between your obsessions and compulsions. Is that really life? It makes me so sad.

There are many environmental reasons that your Obsessive Compulsive Disorder can be triggered. There are certain things or events that might occur throughout your life that can cause an issue. These issues will remain permanent or long term triggers. Some of these issues can be due to an event that happened a long time ago during your childhood. Sometimes they might be from a more recent event. It might be something that happened once or maybe was on-going. It might be a teeny tiny thing to most people. Most people without OCD would not even register a thought about it. To people with OCD, it can be the start of a long term OCD compulsion. Let's examine a few examples.

My first example is an anniversary card. I have a good friend that was an English major. Why is that important? Because she walks around correcting everyone's spelling, grammar and neatness of handwriting. Now you know why I mentioned it. Since I have OCD, it triggers every time I give her a birthday card, anniversary card or a holiday card. She busted me on handwriting a while ago. So, now every time I give her a card and write something on it, I check the crap out of it. I repeatedly check what I wrote over and over. I check to make sure that I spelled everything correctly. The sentences are done correctly and the handwriting is legible. I worry that she will notice and make an issue out of it. This triggers the OCD each and every time I send her a card.

Here is another example. Imagine that you work for a horrible boss. A boss that yells and screams at everything. We all know these types of people. They are definitely out there. Anyway, I had this experience many years ago. Now, what do we know? We know that people with OCD live in constant fear that they will make a mistake or screw something up. It is also layered with the stress and fear and lack of confidence. Due to this, we all tend to be nervous to begin with. So, if you have one of these great bosses, you know that everything must be perfect or what they would call perfect. I was working for one of these types of people. I walked around on eggshells. He went nuts over every little thing. This exacerbated my OCD symptoms. I repeatedly checked everything I did over and over to ensure that it was done correctly. The OCD started on my way to work and was relieved after work. It got worse whenever I was in the boss's office. This is not a specific incident. It was the general stress of dealing with such a mean person and that it skyrocketed my OCD. I was always nervous that I would make a mistake and have to deal with the lunatic's crap. I was sitting in my cubicle and had anxiety for no reason other that I knew I would be dealing with my boss all day. It made going to work extremely unpleasant.

The emotional toll can be difficult to navigate. There are ups and downs. Good days and bad. A lot of the actual depression is a combination of a few different elements. There are medical elements, physical elements and general daily life elements. A lot of my personal OCD comes from the way I live on a day to day basis. Where you are going to get your spicy tuna roll on Tuesday is not that important, right? But to me it is. The fact that the OCD is fake is what makes living with it that much harder. Most people use the phrase, "I can't stop thinking about...". The truth is that someone without OCD can actually stop thinking about it. People with OCD do not have that luxury. When someone with OCD says they cannot stop thinking of something...they really cannot stop thinking of it. It is physically impossible.

Many years of experience will tell you that it seems like someone with OCD has two choices. One, get the thought and do ALL the compulsions. Two, use the behavior therapy. That's where you get the thought and just sit with the lingering obsession and the accompanying anxiety for hours and hours or days and days. Great choices, right? This is a disorder that take so much out of my life. It is an extremely huge part of who I am. I get depressed about it and even cry sometimes when the OCD symptoms are at a high level. I get very tired of doing these ridiculously insignificant things every day. There is a lot of depression living with Obsessive Compulsive Disorder. The depression comes and goes depending on how bad the symptoms are. I have family that know that I have this. I have old friends that I have known most of my life and they do not even know that I have OCD. I live with this secret. It is a secret that everyone with OCD is forced to own.

There is also a lot of sadness knowing that your OCD is affecting others in your life. I have a wonderful Mother that just wants me to be happy. She wants me to live a great life. She has worked very hard to help me. She has spent tons of time researching and researching in order to see if there is a new medication, treatment or type of breakthrough research. It is just as hard for her to watch me live like this as it is for me to actually live like this. She has been there from the beginning of the OCD. She was the only one that was able to figure it out. She took me to all of the doctors. Basically, she too has lost forty years to the pain of Obsessive Compulsive Disorder. This makes me feel unhappy.

There is a lot of angst knowing that my OCD symptoms are affecting the people I love. It hurts them just like it does me. I have tried and tried to control it so it does not bother anyone else. It is EXTREMELY hard to do this. A lot of the time, this ends up in failure. The symptoms always creep back or get strong enough where they are too difficult to hide. That is when the OCD breaks through the behavior therapy. This is what makes living with this so damn hard. You are told by behavior therapists and your family that to control it, you cannot do any of the compulsions. No matter what. By being told over and over that you can control it, you feel like a failure when you cannot. You feel depressed because you are not strong enough to control it. The truth of the matter is that you should not be depressed as many people do the compulsions. Most people try and try, but it does not always work. The reality is that, no matter what your intelligence says, you feel sad and extremely discouraged when you end up succumbing to your Obsessive Compulsive Disorder symptoms. It makes you feel completely and utterly weak.

An example of this is a family vacation to Hawaii. My immediate family and I used to travel every year when my nephews were young. We all love the beach so we chose a vacation based on the beach life. Now remember, the entire point of a vacation is to relax and enjoy the week. This is very easy for most people. We are all usually very excited to spend time with each other. It is a fun time where we can all blow off steam and just enjoy the beach. The great thing about a vacation is that all of us get to leave our usual day to day life at home. It is a great break from the day to day stress of life. On the beach, there are no bills that need to be paid, there are no bosses to listen to, no home repairs, no need to get up early, no emails to send out or respond to, no traffic to sit in, no schedules to abide by and no diets to adhere to. I would think that the OCD would be a lot lower. After all, there are no doors to check, no windows to lock, no cars to lock, no faucets to check, no emails to read over and over, no shopping lists to repeatedly check, no job stress, no computers to make sure are turned off, no computer files to repeatedly save, etc. It seems like I would be very relaxed, right? Not a care in the world. Let's face it, there is nothing for the OCD to do on vacation.

This is not the case for someone with OCD. We cannot just leave the OCD at home. It goes where we go. We cannot just take a vacation from our OCD. It is there all the time no matter what. This vacation example also proves the medical community wrong once again. I have heard over and over that if I do something relaxing, then the OCD will be easier to deal with. Wrong!

No matter where the vacation is, or how nice the beach is, I am not relaxed. I always pack my OCD in my suitcase and take it with me. Needless to say, I need to fight it and use the behavior therapy even on a vacation. As you know, my entire family obviously knows that I have OCD. This means that they are a safe zone. It is safe for me to repeat, check or perform compulsions in front of them. I do not need to hide it. Maybe that is my version of a vacation?

So, I am now on a Hawaiian island sitting on a beautiful beach with a spectacular view of the ocean. There are boats gently floating nearby. There are whales breaching far off in the distance. The weather could not be better. My sister and nephews are swimming in the ocean. I am sitting on the beautiful sand with my Mother. We are both admiring the view. Hmmm...let's see...what should I do? Should I snorkel? Should I surf? Oh, I know, I will repeat ad nauseam. I simply tell my Mother "It would be so nice to be able to live here." She responds with "It would be great." The OCD starts to creep in. I repeat a few times while trying to conceal it. My Mother is an expert on knowing when the OCD is involved. She always knows when it is in play. Needless to say. I continue to repeat. She finally asks me if I am repeating. I say yes. We leave it at that. A little while later, my sister and nephews return from the ocean. It is lunch time.

We begin to pick up our towels and walk back to the condo for lunch. My sister and nephews are walking a little ahead of us. My Mother and I are walking together. I begin to feel like repeating again. I repeat a few more times about how nice it would be to live there. My Mother calmly asks "What is the number?" She obviously is onto the repeating. She knows that it needs to be done a certain number of times. So, I say it is done. We continue walking. We are now in the condo preparing lunch. The urge to repeat returns. I repeat on my Mother again. At this point, I'm sure she wishes that I can just move there and leave her alone.

This is where the emotions get the best of me. I feel very bad that I could not control my OCD. It makes you feel powerless when the OCD affects your life so much. I feel as if I cannot even prepare lunch on a vacation with my family without the OCD chiming in. It can be very depressing. I feel as if I ruined my Mother's vacation or at least a day of it. I am upset that my Mother was nice and calm. She was relaxed and deserves to be. I had to destroy that with my repeating. I felt weak because I could not control it. I felt bad that I could not stick to the behavior therapy. I know I need to use the behavior therapy. It takes being strong. It also takes the ability to continually use it by fighting the OCD tooth and nail every day and every time it shows up. It is difficult. This is why it is so hard to live with it. The feeling is that you will just do the compulsion and get past it. I felt that if I just repeated one last set that it would be great to live in Hawaii, it would be over and I could continue to enjoy the vacation. My Mother would be able to enjoy it as well. Still, I feel horrible. I feel sad that my OCD has, yet again, weaseled its way into our lives. It got so bad that I could not control it. I pushed it that one extra time. I should have just sat with it and this would never have happened. I can now only say that it happened and I need to get past it. Just let it go and move on with the vacation. There are a lot of emotional issues with this disorder. One, that I was not able to fight the OCD and it infiltrated my life. Two, that I was in this situation of do it or not do it once again. I just want to live my life like everyone else. I feel awful. I should be very happy in that beach condo with my family. Instead, I need to fight my brain at every turn. Add that to the list. I cannot just enjoy a vacation. The feeling of sadness and depression hits hard.

Let's use a birthday as another example. I went to my sister's house for her birthday. We just returned from a nice dinner out. It is now time for presents. All of us chipped in on her gift. My nephews handed her the gift. She opened it and loved it. She thanked us all. I quickly have a tiny thought that she does not know it was from me too since I did not actually hand her anything. I quickly say "You know it's from all of us?". She said "I know and thank you." It should have ended there. As per usual, it did not. I felt like I needed to repeat that the gift was from me too. I did it quickly. She said "I got it". I still needed to say it. So, I waited until later. I was washing the dessert dishes with my sister. I repeated it again. She knew it was OCD repeating. She politely responded "Yes, I know. It was from all of you." It made me sad that my OCD symptoms invaded her birthday. Most people would just blow it off. They might say "Forget About It!" because it was nothing. I have even heard "Don't sweat the small stuff." This is all much easier said than done. It is difficult to spend your life facing this type of situation. I have been in this situation over and over and over. The logical side of your brain tells you that the system is fake and who cares about any of it. The physical side tells you a different story. This constant battle is very dark. The thought hits and then the anxiety. Then, your body tells
you that the way out of this situation is by doing the compulsions. You really want to get out of the situation so you perform the compulsions. It is a circular pattern that just plain brings you down.

People in my life that know that I have OCD constantly forward articles or tell me about the new articles they read. There is always something that they want me to try that will supposedly help or cure the OCD. This is never the case. It never works. I have been told by many doctors over the years that exercise is the best way to get rid of the anxiety. It will also give me a break from the thought and that same thought will lower or fade. Guess what? I have been on the treadmill and have had thoughts, anxiety and repeating. I have walked up to five miles in a row. Guess what? Thoughts, repeating, compulsions and anxiety. This happens enough times and you get annoyed and stop listening to advice.

I have tried foods that supposedly help calm and relax someone. I have tried aromas that supposedly help. It is just more baloney. The idea is that you need to relax and stay calm. This will help the OCD. I have tried yoga, strength training, bike riding and massages. I even tried hiring a personal trainer. You know the kind. The type that takes your money and beats you into submission all in the name of fat loss. Get this...during the training sessions while being exhausted...I STILL HAD THE RE-PEATING COMPULSIONS!!!

A life with OCD is different than any other human issue. It is the little things in life that bother me. This is also a part of the problem. The big issues that a person goes through are normal. The little tiny details in life cause the most OCD. This is what makes it so difficult. You never really know if you have handled a detail. This is a source of deep frustration. It is hard to know if you are forcing people in your life to live like they have OCD by the constant repeating to them. I cannot describe how painful this is. I have tried many different things to try to take the edge off. Nothing has worked so far. I have tried to illustrate how someone like me lives like on a day to day basis. It takes a huge emotional toll.

My final thoughts on this is that medical technology moves forward each and every year. There might be a cure at some point. I wanted to show you that there is a lot to deal with. It is NOT all about the physicality of the OCD. It is so much more. If the OCD were to disappear off the face of the earth tomorrow, there would still be a lot of psychological damage to clean up.

The medical community only targets and researches the actual disorder. It is very important to do this. It is also important to fund the research for this type of medical knowledge. The emotional side of this disorder is equally if not more important as well.

If you have OCD, all of this is nothing new to you. I hope that, since I cannot cure you, you were able to seek refuge in that you are not alone. You are not the only person who lives the way you do. If you do not have Obsessive Compulsive Disorder, I hope that this chapter has let you know what someone with OCD goes through. It is a daily burden. There are good days and bad days. Either way, we are Mothers, Fathers, Sisters, Brothers, Sons, Daughters, Cousins, Relatives by marriage, Boyfriends, Girlfriends, etc. The overall point is that we are all in pain. We all struggle. This struggle may lead to anger, sadness, depression and many other emotions. We might not be able to voice our appreciation of everyone in our lives. We may be prone to outbursts due to stress when the OCD and anxiety skyrockets. We are trying the best that we can. On days where this happens it is especially hard. The emotions can be scary. So, please be patient with us.

CHAPTER 12: BEHAVIOR THERAPY!

"Walk Away!"

I have mentioned that medications are used to treat Obsessive Compulsive Disorder. This is the major treatment used for OCD. Each and every one of us, at one point or another, have tried some form of medication. These medications are called "Miracle Drugs" when they first come out. I can tell you from my personal experience that they do not work that great. You need to go to a neurologist or a psychiatrist in order to get a prescription for any of the medications that are used to treat OCD.

The reality of having Obsessive Compulsive Disorder is the same with all of us. We want to find a cure. I am sure that many of us search online to see what is out there and whether or not it actually works. I too have been through this. I have spent endless nights looking to see what is new and improved. I have researched many different drugs. I have also done the research to see if there are any new techniques out there that may work. With OCD, you can spend 70 percent of your daily life doing compulsions or thinking about doing them. This gives you 30 percent of your day to focus and spend on your actual life. The reason we spend the time searching for a possible cure or something that can provide a little bit of relief from the symptoms is due to the fact that if we find something, we can shift the equation. By that, I mean, get 70 percent of our life back and only spend 30 percent of our daily lives catering to the OCD. For that reason, we must always be searching and hoping.

As most doctors will tell you, the medications do not work

perfectly. This means that you have to add another component to complete the treatment for the OCD symptoms. The medication is only about fifty percent of the treatment. The other fifty percent is the knowledge and use of behavior therapy. Behavior therapy in conjunction with the use of medication will provide a much better treatment.

Behavior therapy has a few different names. It might be called Behavior Therapy, Cognitive Behavior Therapy (CBT) or Exposure and Response Therapy. They are all the same thing. They are all designed for the same purpose. They are all expected to be used along with some sort of medication. Most of the doctors that I have been to, have told me that it takes both. You need a medication treatment and the use of behavior therapy to complete the treatment. Basically, the medication does not work alone. It is not good enough. It is only part of the treatment.

The first thing that I can say is that when a doctor who prescribes medication tells you that you need both, that tells you a lot. It tells me that the medications that they will prescribe do not work. The medications have tons of side effects. They will also not work on the OCD. Great huh? The doctor that prescribes the medication actually tells you that they know it will not work. Gee, what confidence! The doctor will also tell you that it is best to try something with the lowest side effects. Another thing you don't want to hear from a doctor. Especially since you are only in their office for a solution and help with your OCD. Anyway, after my OCD exploded on me in my early twenties, I figured it was time to try this, so called, behavior therapy. I found a behavior therapist. Yes, there are specific doctors that teach you behavior therapy. I researched one and made an appointment.

I will do my best to walk you through the overall entire process. The idea behind the behavior therapy is that you are training yourself to not do the compulsions when the OCD occurs. Once you master this, then you can use it against all aspects of the OCD. The basic idea of behavior therapy is a very easy premise to understand: JUST DON'T DO IT! That's it. Sounds easy enough, right? It sounds much easier that it actually is. The goal is to not do any of the compulsions. No matter what, do not do any of them. It is much easier said that done. As someone with OCD can tell you, it is NOT an easy process. Behavior therapy is based on the one fact of: <u>do not do it</u>. The overall idea is to not react to the OCD thoughts or compulsions. Basically, you are training yourself to completely ignore the OCD and all of its processes. You need to try to ignore a huge part of your life. You practice ignoring your biggest asset: your brain. The idea is whenever you get a thought or a feeling, you do nothing. If you feel that you need to do a compulsion, you do nothing. If you have anxiety, you do nothing. If you get a feeling or obsessive thought - too bad. Here is another fun fact, you actually spend time triggering the OCD. Yep, you read that correctly, YOU TRIGGER YOUR OCD!!! This brings it on so you can practice ignoring it. With OCD, you spend your entire life trying very hard to make sure that your symptoms do not get triggered. Behavior Therapy is designed to hold back your OCD so that you can then learn to deal with it. This is done by practicing ignoring the thoughts and not doing the compulsions. This includes both the light thoughts and the hard core issues. The entire therapy is based on one major thing…your reaction to your own brain's signals and what it tells you. This is not easy. The worst part is that with OCD, you fall into the pattern of getting a thought and reacting towards the OCD. This is where your brain is trained to automatically send a thought and you to instantly react. Your brain tells you that you need to say something three times and you are trained to do it. The Obsessive Compulsive Disorder has you trained to do what it says…PERIOD!!! This is why you always will do it. No matter what, you will just keep doing it and doing it. Behavior therapy is designed to unwind that thought process. To basically go against the grain. You need to be strong and not do what you feel you need to do. You have to go against every feeling in your body. It is difficult but can be done.

The behavior therapy has a few different pieces to it. There is exposure, response and avoidance. The exposure piece is where you are meant to trigger the OCD. You do whatever is needed to trigger a thought, feeling, anxiety or compulsion. The bottom line is that you run towards whatever causes an OCD issue in your life. The response is exactly that...your response. Your response is where you simply ignore the thought, feeling, anxiety or compulsion. You overall ignore the OCD. You respond to the uncomfortable feelings by simply not doing a thing to remedy it. Absolutely no compulsions can be done. The avoidance is a piece of the OCD lifestyle. People will OCD tend to avoid doing, saying or going to certain places. This is due to the fact that you are avoiding an action that you know from past history is a trigger for your OCD. A small example is that if you get a bad thought every time you chew gum, plain and simple, you never chew gum. The basic idea is that you avoid what causes the OCD to flare up. You know, just by living, what these triggers are and what causes your OCD. After a while, you know exactly what will set off the OCD. This makes you just avoid those things due to the stress of having to deal with the OCD and its many compulsions. This is where the term "Avoidance" comes from. Avoidance is not allowed with behavior therapy. You need to face your demons head on! Now that you are up to speed on the idea of behavior therapy, we can move on.

I will try to explain and give you an idea of what to expect when dealing with a behavior therapist and the process that is needed to learn cognitive behavior therapy. Within the first few sessions, your therapist will have you make a list of all of your OCD symptoms. This might not be a physical list as the therapist may just talk to you about each symptom. The therapist will go through the daily OCD symptoms that you have. They will ask you to explain the anxiety and compulsions that are attached to each symptom. This list is basically a smallest to largest list. If you prefer, call it an easiest to hardest list. The smallest/easiest symptoms are the issues with the least amount of anxiety and compulsions. They are the easiest to sit through. The hardest/ largest symptoms are those symptoms that have the most anxiety and compulsions. They are the hardest to sit though. Basically, you are rating your day to day obsessions and compulsions. This lets the therapist know which symptoms are hard for you to deal with and which are not that bad. The list will show your obsessions and compulsions starting with the small ones and gradually growing to the most difficult. This list is very helpful and will give the therapist a starting point.

The behavior therapist will use the OCD symptom list to create weekly assignments for you to follow through with. These assignments will need to be done between your weekly therapy sessions. The assignments have one major point to them. This point is to trigger the OCD and cause you to deal with it. The idea is to train you how to respond to the OCD. The assignments will train you how to react when the OCD is triggered...Period!!!

The assignments are designed a few different ways. The therapist will structure assignments with you. The therapist will begin the assignments with the issues that cause you the least amount of problems. Basically, they will begin with the easy obsessions, anxiety and compulsions. Each assignment will include a few parts. The first is a task that you and your therapist will decide on. This is the task that will literally set off the OCD. It will definitely include something that causes you an OCD issue. This will be an issue that you have already mentioned to the therapist as a particular problem. The next part will be a progress sheet. The progress sheet will list the task, a number from one to ten and a conclusion. The one to ten is for you to write down and document what level the anxiety was during the entire task. The progress sheet will also include a conclusion sheet. The conclusion is basically how the assignment went. These notes will be handed back to your therapist on the next session. There will usually be three or so assignments in between each session.

I will give you an example of how the assignments work. Let's say, you mention to the therapist that you get an obsession that you have contracted a disease from simply touching the front door of the local coffee house. The assignment will be geared towards this specific obsession. The assignment will be to go to the coffee shop. Then, well, walk in by pushing/touching the front door of the coffee house. The obsession will, as usual and quite predictably, EXPLODE!!! This is where the real behavior therapy comes in. You will be shocked with the thought and immediately bombarded with the anxiety. The behavior therapy assignment will be to just sit and "enjoy" your coffee. You will do nothing. No reaction whatsoever. You cannot stand by the door or even look at the door. You simply touch the door and "WALK AWAY"!!! You then just have to "sit" in the feeling. No matter what…. you need to sit in it. It will be difficult. The difficulty comes from the logic that what you are thinking is, in no way, possible in reality. It will also be difficult due to the anxiety. Then there is the anxiety caused by even having anxiety. Having fun yet? The final reason this will be difficult is because, for the first time, you are actually going against the OCD and doing the opposite of what your entire life with OCD has taught you. Remember, you are trained to automatically do the compulsion. This is why you need behavior therapy in the first place. This is the first time that you are trying to turn the tide. This alone will cause stress and even more anxiety. Let's say that the compulsion for this particular obsession is to touch the front door again. The science of anxiety is that it will naturally go away or subside within two hours time. So, you will stay in the coffee house for two hours and the assignment will be completed. Upon leaving, you still cannot do the compulsion when you touch the door on the way out. This can be done with a little trickery. All you have to do is to take out your phone as if you just got a silent call. So, your phone is in one hand and your coffee is in the other. So, with your hands being full, you can walk out by leaning your back against the door. The compulsion will, most likely, include the "way" that you touch the door i.e. with your actual hands. Since, you leaned into the door to push it open, you did not use your hands so technically, you did not do the compulsion. This further completes the assignment. Plus, you did not act weird as no one will even notice anything. They will just think you are a very busy person and, like everyone else, you live on your phone. Then you go home and write the information down for your therapist. Great job!

Let's look at another example. For this example, we will use checking the front door a certain number of times. Imagine that the OCD tells you that the door is not locked if you do not check the front door five times. The obsession will be that the front door is wide open. You may even get a few fun visuals of this. Maybe a visual of you coming home and the front door is open so all of your stuff was stolen and your house is empty. The anxiety will follow. The further you get away from the house, the more likely the door will be open. The anxiety will build and build. The assignment will require you to go out the front door and only check it once. The OCD will explode. As soon as it does, you do nothing. You simply "WALK AWAY!". Just leave the front door alone and go out somewhere. Maybe you can go get some coffee and double up on the assignments. Just kidding! Actually, the point is to sit with the feeling that the door is not locked. Then do nothing. That is the exposure and response. Trigger the OCD to expose yourself and respond by doing nothing and "WALK AWAY!" In this particular assignment. I find it helpful to mock the OCD. This can be done by saying to yourself, "Oh well, I guess everything I own will be stolen. Too bad. The good news is that I can use the insurance money and be able to by all new stuff with better features.", Basically, "Screw you OCD!" The assignment will require you to not do the compulsion and go out for about two hours. Remember, the research indicates that the anxiety will disappear or lessen within about two hours. So, you go out for the two hours to complete the assignment. Then you come home and write the results down on the assignment progress sheet to document it for your therapist. This will let them know how the assignment went. Congratulations, you have just completed another assignment.

Let's do one more example of an assignment that involves the popular avoidance. If you recall, avoidance is the act of, well, avoidance. That is to say that you avoid doing something that you are sure will start or trigger the OCD. For this example, I will use avoiding a street. Imagine that there is a street in your neighborhood that you hate driving down. There are always children playing, adults on bikes and animals. Every time that you drive down this particular street, you get an obsession that you have hit someone or something. So, since the street is in your neighborhood, you see it every day. With OCD, you get very good at avoiding something that will trigger the OCD. So, naturally, you avoid driving down this street. You do this by taking the long way and spending a few more minutes to get home. Anything it takes to not drive down that street. You avoid it completely. The behavior therapist will give you an assignment for this. Want to guess what it is? Yup, you're right! Drive down that street. The therapist will give you an assignment where you drive down that street once. You will not be able to drive back around the other way so that you can "Check" to see if you hit anything. You will basically drive down the street and keep going. Remember 'WALK AWAY!' or in this case "DRIVE AWAY!". Just drive down the street once and sit with the obsession, visuals and anxiety that you hit something or someone. Then you go home and wait about two hours. It's now time to record the results for the therapist on the sheet of paper. Are you starting to get the idea?

I have given you some examples to show you how the behavior therapy works. Now, I will tell you my specific story of my journey through behavior therapy. I went to a behavior therapist when I was twenty-two. At the time, I was not on any medication. So, I did it without that help. A few of the assignments were easy and some were a lot more difficult. I learned some great techniques that I still use today. I learned some good things and some bad things. I will try to describe them both to you.

I researched the local behavior therapists and made an appointment. I had no idea what to expect. This was the first time that I would set foot in the world of behavior therapy. I knew that I had to do something as my OCD was very high. I knew that the therapist would teach me how to go against my OCD. This is something that I have never done before. I was motivated as I would get rid of some of the OCD and learn to deal with it. I was nervous, but at the same time, was looking forward to it.

I showed up at the time of the appointment. The therapist worked out of a clinic that specialized in anxiety. All types of anxiety disorders. I walked in and sat down on a chair. I waited and then the therapist came out and said that he was ready. I walked into his office. I was nervous as I did not know what to expect. He explained the process which is what I started this chapter with. The idea is not to do it no matter what. In other words, "WALK AWAY!" You get the idea.

He asked me to explain some of my symptoms. This is the listing of the symptoms that I mentioned earlier. We discussed the symptoms for a while. He gave me a few pointers in order to succeed. He wanted to ensure that the assignments were successful. He provided me with some suggestions on how to perform the behavior therapy. These were ideas on how to go against the OCD. They were little techniques and tricks to do the behavior therapy. Remember, the golden rule, always do the opposite of what the OCD says. After all, the behavior therapist has a lot of experience accumulated from all of the patients that he has seen. This gives you a good shot at being successful. These little tips and tricks became very useful.

I started my first assignment while house sitting. The assignment involved the garage door. I always had a problem when I left the house with closing the garage door. I would get into my car, turn the car on, and back out of the garage. Once I was out of the garage, I would push the garage door remote for it to close. I literally saw the door close, right in front of my eyes. I am now sitting in my car, looking at a garage door that is completely closed. I can see it, touch it, bang on it, kick it, and anything else to prove that it is closed. Then, like everyone else, I should simply drive away. There is one problem. I don't know if you know this or not by reading this book, but I have OCD! So naturally, the second that I turn my head to back out of the driveway, I have no clue as to whether I shut the garage door or not. Any guesses as to what the assignment for this was? Yup, you guessed it! The assignment was to pull out of the garage. Then push the button for the door to close. The OCD thoughts and visuals of the door still being wide open will start accompanied by some much hated anxiety. The feeling of something being incomplete also hits. Then, I am to just leave. Do not look at the door, through the rearview mirror, out the back window, etc. Just leave without knowing if the garage door was shut or not. In other words: "DRIVE AWAY!" Like "WALK AWAY!" - get it? I then leave the house for about two hours. I go to have coffee at a local coffee house. I drive there, park my car, go into the shop, wait on line and order my coffee. This is all while having the existing visuals and feelings that I did not close the garage door at all. The feeling was, that while I was drinking my coffee, the door was wide open. I could see the visual in my mind. It was like I was actually standing there looking at a wide open garage door. So there I am, sitting at the coffee shop and drinking my coffee. The entire time, I am thinking about the garage door. To the other patrons, I look nice and relaxed. The reality is that I am still nervous about the garage door. I have anxiety over it. The obsession is still lingering. I am still uncomfortable and on edge. I still have to sit there for two hours. As I do, I notice something interesting; the thought and the feeling is lowered a little bit. It is not as easy as my first assignment. It took a lot to do this assignment. This is the first time I went against the OCD hardcore. The first time I ignored it. The first time I sat in the thought. The first time I did not do what the force of habit was; which was doing the compulsion. This was the first time I actually just sat and did nothing. It is very weird for me. The thought gets a little lower and lower. After the two hours is up, I am free to go back to the house. I finish my coffee, get into my car and drive all the way there. Guess what I find? The garage door is completely closed and locked. I am excited. I run in the house and document it on the progress sheet. I have completed the assignment. I am still unsure about the behavior therapy, but I am glad that I finished the first assignment.

I then began assignment number two. The same problem that I had with the garage door was also happening with any faucet in my place. This assignment involved the kitchen sink. I would wash the dishes. I would then turn the faucet off and walk out of the room. Then the obsession would hit. I immediately felt that I did not turn the faucet off and that water was still pouring out of the faucet. I knew that this was not true. I knew that I had closed the faucet correctly. The obsession gave me a visual that there was water pouring out of the faucet. Even though I knew that there wasn't. I could also not hear any water dripping. I still felt that the faucet was on. This assignment: I had to turn the faucet on, turn the faucet off and leave the room for two hours. I could do nothing. Do not check it. Do not look back at it. Just "WALK AWAY!". I went upstairs for two hours and turned on the TV. The thought, the anxiety, and the obsession lingered for the entire time. The visual got worse. The visuals started out with the fact that the faucet was just running. Then they moved to the sink being clogged and the water pouring out of the basin. Basically, while I was upstairs watching TV, the entire kitchen floor was being covered with water. This went on for about two hours. The thought did get a little lower and lower. Once again, I ignored the OCD. I did not react to it. I did not double check. I did not do the compulsion. I did not fear the thought. I did not react to the thought. I did absolutely nothing. I did not do what my mind was telling me to do. I did not fall for the force of habit which was to do the compulsion automatically. I just: "WALKED AWAY!" After the two hours, I went downstairs. As you can imagine, the faucet was completely closed and the floor was completely dry. I documented the assignment on the progress sheet for the behavior therapist. I completed this second assignment.

For the next assignment, I will use the repeating. One of my major symptoms, is in fact, repeating. When the OCD is high, then the repeating is high. I repeat some sentences over and over. This is where the therapist gave me some tips and tricks on how to use the behavior therapy. He told me that when repeating kicked up, do not repeat. The way this is done is to just say something once and then not repeat it no matter what. Naturally I was talking to a coworker and felt the urge to repeat. I then had to begin the assignment. This was done by finishing the conversation without repeating. This was a conversation version of "WALK AWAY!" I had to sit with the feeling that I did not finish repeating. The obsession got stronger and stronger. The feeling got stronger and stronger. The anxiety got stronger and stronger. I really felt like I needed to repeat to my coworker. I had to unexpectedly, start a new work assignment. I did it by finishing the conversation without repeating. I went back to my desk and began working. The feeling, thought and anxiety remained. I sat for about two hours and completed the assignment. Once again, I went against the OCD. I did not do the compulsion. I did not fall for the force of habit. I went against everything in my body to not repeat. It was difficult. The obsession was that I was trapped in a set of numbers. The feeling that something was not quite finished got even stronger and stronger. It was not fun. I sat and distracted myself with work for the two hours. It was not easy. I noticed that the feeling stayed for the two hours. I did not do the repeating. I completed the assignment. I documented it on the progress sheet for the therapist.

The next assignment was geared towards the numbers. I have the wonderful life of living in numbers. So, the therapist suggested that we hit the numbers. The entire point of the behavior therapy, in terms of the numbers, is to not do them. The basic idea is to not do the compulsion. This is done by purposely doing the task the "Wrong" number of times. So, if you feel that you need to do something four times, purposely do it three or five times. I was at work and was in the file room. I opened a drawer one time and took a file out. I got the information that I needed from the file. I closed the drawer. I immediately felt that I needed to open and close the drawer four more times to make three sets of two. I knew it was time for the assignment. Now remember, I opened the drawer once to take the file out and closed it to put the file back. This was a total of one set. I decided to begin the assignment. I needed to do it two more times to make it three sets. I ignored the OCD. I did not do the compulsion. I simply "WALKED AWAY!" I went back to my desk. I sat for the two hours. I had anxiety and thought that I needed to complete the set of three. I felt like I was trapped in the set of numbers. I felt like something was incomplete. This thought lingered. After the two hours, I was done with the assignment. I documented it on my progress sheet for my therapist. I completed this assignment. Are you getting the idea of how the therapy works?

The final assignment I will discuss was with checking my car. I would drive somewhere and park my car. I would then turn my car off. I would get out of the car. I would lock the door. Then I would continue on my way. The OCD would start. The obsession is that I did not lock my car and it will be stolen. This would cause me to do the compulsion and check the car a certain number of times. I mentioned this to the therapist. It was time for an assignment. The assignment was to lock the door and "WALK AWAY!" I began the assignment. I parked in the parking lot. I got out of my car. I locked the door and "WALKED AWAY!" The obsession and anxiety kicked in. After work, I came back to the parking lot. Sure enough, my car was there perfectly intact. I documented the first two hours for the therapist on the progress sheet. I completed this assignment.

If you've read my chapter entitled "Feeding Time", then you know how easy it is to "feed" the OCD. By feeding it, it grows.

By not feeding it, it goes. The more you feed it, the worse it gets. The less you feed it, the easier it gets. The more you do it, the more you will do it. The less you do it, the less you will do it.

Let's examine the way that it grows. If you check something three times, then you can also check anything else three times. The numbers are also part of it. If you check something 5 times, then you can check anything five times. The OCD will move from one thing to another. Once you give in to the OCD on one thing, you will, most likely, start to give in on other items as well. You get the idea? See how this works? The more compulsions that you do, the more compulsions there will be to do. That is how it grows. It is your basic snowball effect.

Let's examine the way it lowers. It is the exact opposite of the way that it grows. The way to lower the OCD is to break up the control and the process of the compulsions. You need to crush it every time it hits. The way to lower it is to reverse the process. It is not easy, but it can be done.

Here is the idea. If you do not do one thing, then you will not need to do another. If you do not need to check something, you will not need to check anything else. You need to unwind the OCD slowly. If you don't check one thing, then why check another? Basically, it is the exact opposite of feeding it. You will begin to get used to smashing it. You will begin doing the compulsions less and less. It will become easier and you will get good at it. The reality is that you will do less and less of the compulsions. The less that you do them, the less that you will need to do them.

My experience with the behavior therapy was pretty good. I learned a lot. I still use the behavior therapy today. I got to understand that it works pretty well. The behavior therapist was excellent. I went for about six months. The sessions were once a week. Like everything else, there were ups and downs.

THE BAD NEWS! I will start with the bad news. The bad news about behavior therapy is that it does not work well with-

out the proper medication and the proper dose of the medication. It is difficult to be successful without medication. This is
why most doctors will tell you that you need both medication
and behavior therapy. This is the only way to be somewhat in
control. In my experience, the behavior therapy did not work
without the medication. I had a ton of anxiety which always
made it difficult to perform the behavior therapy. The behavior
therapy will only work when the thought is light. The thought
is only light when the anxiety is low. I also began the behavior
therapy when the OCD was explosive and high. It was everywhere. This made it especially difficult as it felt like I was chip-
ping away at something so huge that was controlling me. It felt
as if I would never get hold of it. I had a lot of anxiety at that
time. It was not easy to handle. I was not able to do the behavior
therapy perfectly. I felt as if I was swimming upstream. It was
a very difficult time for me. The OCD started the second I woke
up and lasted all day until I went to sleep. It was everywhere. I
worked at the behavior therapy every chance that I had. It was
not an easy task. I tried and tried and the thoughts, feelings, visuals and anxiety were everywhere. Without medication, it was
very hard for me to dig myself out from under.

There is another problem with behavior therapy. You have
to do it all the time. It must be done every day and with every
obsession or compulsion. You need to perform it from the moment you wake up to the moment you fall asleep. You have to
do it every single time the OCD rears its head. It is difficult to
do it every single time that it hits. It does not matter if it is a
small force of habit or a large scale full blown obsession; you still
need to use the behavior therapy techniques to try and control
it. The higher the OCD, the more difficult it is to do the behavior
therapy.

There was another issue that I had with the behavior therapy. It took the same amount of time out of my life as doing the
actual compulsions. Here is why. If you have a thought and the
compulsion is to check a door or repeat; the behavior therapist

will tell you to "Sit" in the thought no matter how long it lasts. To do so, you simply do nothing about it. So, you just "Sit" in it. But the thought does not necessarily go away. Now, as we all know, the compulsion is attached to the thought. The compulsion is what "Stops" the thought or at least gives the illusion that it will. So, with OCD, you usually start doing the compulsion. You already know that by doing it, you feed the OCD. So, in effect, the thought will stay longer and the compulsions will go into the numbers. The point being that the compulsions will last a few hours. Instead, you are stuck "Sitting" with a thought, anxiety and visuals that lasts a few hours. The bottom line is that you are trading one uncomfortable feeling for another. The fact of the matter is that no matter what, you will lose a few hours or days out of your life whether or not you do the behavior therapy. The behavior therapy just gives you a choice of how you want to waste the next few hours of your life. The choice being sitting there and trying to distract yourself, or doing a ton of compulsions. The fact of the matter is that there are so many obsessions and compulsions to do that it is very difficult to use the behavior therapy. It is always playing catch up. You do one and ten more pop up. You solve one issue and four more arrive. You use the behavior therapy on one obsession and it does not work on another. Another issue is that you have to have endurance. You need to do it every day for the rest of your life. It is easy to do it for a day or two. It is much more difficult to use it every day of one's life. No matter what, it is a lifelong commitment. Whenever the OCD starts to creep up again, you need to do the behavior therapy. It will never stop and neither can you. It is not easy to practice it every second of every day. You get very tired of having to fight yourself. The bottom line is that the behavior therapy does not work without medication.

THE GOOD NEWS! I went on medication. I saw a neurologist and he prescribed Zoloft. I started the medication. A few weeks later, I noticed something interesting. The behavior therapy had begun to work. I was able to "Sit" with the thoughts

without doing the compulsions. I noticed that it had gotten easier and easier to crush the OCD. I also noticed that it was longer
and longer in between the obsessions. This was due to the behavior therapy and the medication both working. I was able to
use the behavior therapy on more and more compulsions. I was
able to not do some compulsions at all. As far as the numbers
and sets, I was able to either not do them or do them incorrectly
and be fine with that. I did not care what number I had landed or
finished on. I did not care if it was a good or right number or a
bad or wrong number. I just did not care. Then the behavior therapy got easier and easier. I would willfully go against the OCD.
For the first time, I was in control. Sometimes, I would purposely
do things incorrectly, the wrong way or the opposite of what my
brain was telling me. It felt great. I felt so happy to be able to
smash it. I did not fear the OCD hitting me. I did not fear the anxiety which was low, due to the medication. I was not afraid to do
or say things. I was not trapped in the OCD rules and regulations.
I felt more confident than I ever did before. The thoughts and
feelings kept dissipating. When they appeared, then went away
rather quickly. I got to the point that I was happy to do things
throughout the day. I was able to smash everything that came
my way. The behavior therapy was finally working. For the first
time in my life, I was in charge.

The overall premise of behavior therapy is a good one. The
idea of not listening to the annoying voice of Obsessive Compulsive Disorder is great. It is a very important part of living with
the OCD. You will find it very useful. The only problem is that it
will only work and give you the freedom you desire when it is in
combination with the proper medication and the proper dose.

The way I look at it is that the OCD is a lifelong thing. I
am in for the long hall. Even with the medication, the behavior
therapy is not always easy. I have to practice it every second the
OCD hits. It is difficult to sustain. I feel that the combination of
the medication and the behavior therapy is good overall. I will
have seventy percent of my life and thirty percent of the time

spent on the OCD. That is much better than having thirty percent of my life and seventy percent of the time spent on OCD. I would recommend choosing a medication and trying that prior to going to a behavior therapist. It will make your life a whole lot easier. The behavior therapy does not work perfectly. I do not think anything will be a perfect treatment. Let's face it, there is no real fix, as of yet, for someone who suffers from Obsessive Compulsive Disorder. It is better to do the behavior therapy than not. The behavior therapy is a good thing and it has helped me. All and all, the behavior therapy should be considered part of the life with OCD. That's it.

CHAPTER 13: MEDICATIONS!

"1 + 1 = Zoloft!"

Medication or usually known as a quick fix. PILLS! PILLS! AND MORE PILLS! The medical community must have established that medication is the only way to help someone with OCD. If someone is sedated and relaxed, they might leave the doctors alone and go away. This is why there is a medication to "fix" everything. You're under a lot of stress at work? Take a pill! You are depressed while going through a messy divorce? Take a pill! You have high blood pressure? Take a pill! Your kids eat donuts, potato chips and wash it down with a sugar filled soda? Surprisingly, they have trouble paying attention. They get labeled ADHD and guess what? They take a pill! There are pills for everything now. And why not, the pharmaceutical companies are making billions over people's life long suffering. Well, OCD is no different in the eyes of the medical/pharmaceutical business. Guess what all you OCD sufferers... that's right...there's a pill for it!

Here's the problem: All of these medications have tons of side effects. Then you need to get more pills to fix what the first drug caused. If you have an itch in your right foot, you go to the doctor. He says that you need (funny drug names inserted here) physogrit. You pay the doctor a few hundred due to the fact that your Health Care Plan or as I call it "Health Don't Care Plan", does not cover that foot doctor. Anyway, you go down to the local pharmacy where you need to show ID for any medication and fill the foot doctor's prescription. After a few weeks of the physogrit, you have a dry mouth. So, you go to the mouth doctor.

He says you need tryoslet. So, it's back to the pharmacy. A few more weeks of the physogrit and the tryoslet and you develop diarrhea. The butt doctor says to take buttohex. Back to the pharmacy. A few weeks of the physogrit, tryoslet and buttohex and you still have the itch in your right foot. Only now, you also have a dry mouth and diarrhea. So on and so on. The overall point is that you will end up on several different medications and might still have the original problem. Gee these pharmaceuticals are great. And yup, OCD is no different.

There are many different medications claiming to at least lower the OCD. They are supposed to make the symptoms manageable. They are in the category of a Selective Serotonin Reuptake Inhibitor or SSRI for short. Most of them are either anti-depressants or designed to work like one. They are designed to increase the serotonin in your brain but it does not feel like the serotonin increases in your body. Serotonin is the "Happy" juice in the brain. It is supposedly why we feel happy, calm, low anxiety, etc. Low serotonin is believed to be one cause of OCD, Tourette's Syndrome and many other conditions. It is believed that a person's serotonin levels have to be in a certain range to be happy and without crippling anxiety. Not too high and not too low. If you have low serotonin, you develop these issues. If you have high serotonin, you develop other issues. The basic idea of these medications is to adjust your serotonin. With the new adjustment, the brain will get what it needs. Then, supposedly, you will be happy and have minimal OCD. That is why anti-depressants are used for OCD sufferers.

The medical community must have done a lot of research and noticed that most people with OCD are depressed. So, needless to say, most OCD drugs contain some sort of anti-depression mixture. Basically, a happy pill. There are a couple of medications that are not specifically designed to work on OCD. They have been tested here and there over the years. At some point, they figured out that these medications might actually "work" on someone with OCD. It might not be the full intent of the pharmaceutical companies to produce a drug for OCD sufferers specifically. So sometimes a cocktail of drugs is used. If they find out that the mixture possibly works on OCD, then they call their marketing department and tell them to get to work so they can make millions more on their new treatment. They consider it two birds with one stone. Point being, there are tons of options for drugs that may or may not work. Some specifically for OCD and others not. Great odds huh?

There are a few main medications that are for OCD sufferers. For those of us that have done the research, we all know how horrible they are. I'm sure you have heard of these. Either from online research, a doctor or your favorite sitcom that says it to insult the lovable idiot character on the show. Each have a brand version and a generic version. If you go to a neurologist, they will give you a rundown of each medication. They can also recommend the dosage that you should be on. They make it sound great. Then reality sets in and you decide to do a quick online search on the medication. Never a good thing. You will find a blogs from all over the world. As you skim through these blog entries, you will soon realize that a lot of people are having a lot of different side effects. That is, if the medication even helped them at all. The people who post to those are curious to see if it works with anyone else and are trying to determine if they should just stick with it. Most, I'm sure, are in the same position as most of us who tried the medications. To struggle with it and see if it can possible work. The age old struggle of "Can I live like this?".

As for me, I will do my best to describe my personal experiences with the medications. I was 18 years old and my Mother and I decided to see what was out there in terms of chemical warfare with the OCD. I met my first neurologist. I went for blood tests and to discuss the possibilities. This was in 1989. At that time, there were tons of articles always referring to these new OCD curing drugs as "Miracle" drugs. The doctor explained that Anafranil was the best choice as there were virtually no major side effects. I decided to try Anafranil. I tried it and sure enough, a few months later and I was a walking zombie. I was tired and starting to become overweight. I was too tired to do anything. This was not good. My mother noticed a big difference in my personality. We decided to discontinue the drug.

It is now 1999 and I was 28 years old. I was working for an entertainment company and had my own apartment. I went back to school to get a business degree and had just finished. I worked in an office so naturally my symptoms were horrible. As most of my fellow OCD people can tell you, an office is a perfect place for OCD to live and to grow. There is constant stress. OCD also has the added benefit of a feeling of low self-esteem. There is also a constant feeling of fear that you will screw something up. Given that, the OCD flourishes in the workplace. There are plenty of files, forms, computer databases, contracts and memos to check, double check, re-check, triple check and re-check the double check. This is VERY time consuming, not to mention the toll it takes on your life. In an office building, there are tons and tons of elevators to push buttons a certain number of times, offices to walk in and out of, files rooms with tons of file cabinets to repeatedly open, bathrooms with faucets that need turning off and a parking lot to complete checking your car to make sure that it is locked. All of this takes time away from actually working. This makes you slow, careful, nervous and unable to perform the way that your bosses will want. The bottom line is that WORKING WITH OCD SUCKS...PERIOD!!! It became hard to do my job and I was miserable. I was VERY unhappy. I was in need of some sort of relief. I had a job to do and was determined to succeed. I need to try to figure out a way to get rid of or lower my OCD.

I decided to revisit the medication scene thinking that, like technology, the medication field had been very busy, OCD was starting to become well known, so naturally were are bigger and better drugs out there. There were a lot. Some new and others old and trustworthy. I will only tell you about Zoloft as that was my drug. Please remember that this is just my personal experience and no one else's.

I went to a university medical center that specialized in testing and working with the new OCD drugs. I was asked about my symptoms and was told that Zoloft was the best medication out there as it had the least amount of side effects compared to its competition. It was the only medication with basically no side effects. It is one of the anti- depressant medications that I mentioned with some properties that might have an effect on OCD. It is not an OCD drug nor is it designed specifically for it. It is a drug that might work with OCD so it is prescribed for such. I guess the idea is that, as an anti-depressant, it lowers the anxiety as well as makes you feel a little better or "Happy" about your life. I guess the thought is that you will feel so good that you will be able to use behavior therapy as a weapon and smash the OCD. I received a prescription and went happily on my way.

I filled the prescription at my local pharmacy. I was given a very low dose to start off. I was on 5 milligrams. The average dose was 75 milligrams and up. The FDA set a ceiling of the daily total at 200 milligrams. I was nervous as I had no idea if it would work. I was also not too happy to take medications given my prior experience.

I took the first dose on the first night and went to bed. I woke up the next morning. Surprisingly, I still had OCD. Sorry, that dramatic buildup was fun for me. As we all know, nothing works right away especially with such a low dose. A breath mint has more medication in it that 5 milligrams. About two weeks later, I went back to the doctor as a check point. They mainly wanted to make sure my teeth had not fallen out from the medi-cation. Yup, still had teeth so it was time to increase the dose. I do not want to bore you with the day to day and week to week in-creases. Just know that this was the process.

I was now up to 75 milligrams. AHA! I noticed a difference. It was small, but given my past history with OCD, I gladly embrace it. I began to notice that my anxiety was a little lower. I was gaining weight from the medication, but who cares. Getting rid of the OCD was much more important. I went back to the doctors and they increased it to 100 milligrams, 125 milligrams and then 150 milligrams. At this point, I began to notice that the anxiety was much lower and the behavior therapy was beginning to work. I began smashing away at every thought, feeling, vision and yes...the numbers. It felt great. I was beginning to get my life back. I began to increase more and more. I was now up to the famous 200 milligrams.

I was doing much better. I was not perfect, but had the ability to function more. It became easier and easier to stand up to the OCD. I was going in the right direction but still could use more of an edge. My weight had increased a lot, but I still didn't care. My freedom was more important. I got the okay from the Doctors to increase to 250 milligrams. This was big as it was 50 milligrams above the recommended dose. As I mentioned, I purposely chose a university where they push the dosage of the medication to get the full potential. They really were ahead of the curve and way ahead of the rest of the world.

I was now on the 250 for a few weeks. It felt awesome! I was finally able to function more like a human. I felt much happier due to the anti-depressant properties. I felt good enough to try the behavior therapy. I felt to check my front door three times. Perfect time to see if this stuff works. I decided to check the front door twice. I sat there for a minute to see if there were any results. The first thing that I noticed was that the anxiety was lower when I had the feeling that something was not done "Correctly". I had a feeling to keep checking it. The anxiety was lower than usual. I thought for a second and decided to try sitting through it. The thought was there. It was much lighter and less in your face and the anxiety was not consuming me. It was actually a weird feeling to be able to sit through it. I distracted myself by continuing on with my night. I had dinner, took a shower and watched some TV. It was about an hour or so when, all of a sudden, I realized...HEY! I did not check my door the "Right" number of times. The anxiety was gone and the thought faded. SUCCESS! I decided that I needed to use the behavior therapy as much as possible and see what happens.

I woke up the next morning when my alarm went off. I was determined to crush the OCD and once and for all, free myself from this nightmare. I began smashing all thoughts and feelings. I used all of the rules that I was taught from the behavior therapist a few years prior. I started with the numbers. I purposely did things the wrong number of times. If I felt to do something three times, I would do it any other number such as 1,2,4,5,6, etc. ANYTHING BUT THREE!!! If I got a thought, I would ignore it. A feeling? Ignore it! Anxiety? Ignore it! I began using behavior therapy in all aspects of my life. The behavior therapy became increasingly easier and easier over the next few months. You already know from the prior chapter "Behavior Therapy" what it was like trying to control the OCD without the medication. Now, I will show you what it's like with the medication.

I am now at work. I had my morning coffee and went through some emails to see what needed a response. It's now around 9:45am and I have a meeting at 10:00am. I go into the company computer system and print a few contract reports out. I am now ready for the meeting. A thought slowly enters in the form of doubt. I am not sure if I printed the right reports that my boss specifically asked for in the meeting. This will not go over well if I am missing them in the meeting. I quickly double check the stack of reports and it is there. I go back to my coffee. As you know, a few seconds later, the thought comes back. "Did I print the right reports?", "Will I look like an idiot in front of everyone?", "Will the boss yell at me during the meeting in front of my co-workers?" I know that I checked the stack of reports. I know that I printed the right reports. I know they are correct. With the Zoloft, the anxiety is much lower and the thoughts are weaker. So, I just thought, "Who cares if the reports are wrong and who cares if the boss yells at me. I will just slip out of the meeting and print what I need and run back into the conference room. No big deal." I sat with the thought for a minute while finishing my coffee. The thought soon faded and I was, again, relaxed, calm, and ready for my meeting. As you can guess, the meeting went very smoothly as the reports were obviously correct.

I continued to work. There were many other thoughts that I was able to destroy before lunch. I felt to get into the elevator the right number of times. I did not. I had to shake a co-workers hand a few times. I did not. I had to email people a certain number of times. I did not. I felt that I screwed something up. I just kept going. I needed to print something prior to lunch. I hit the print icon. A message came up on the printer that it was out of toner. I went into the supply cabinet and grabbed a sealed toner cartridge. I opened the package. I removed the old printer cartridge from the printer and placed it in the recycler. As I am doing this, my finger slightly grazes the part of the cartridge that has black toner dust on it. I replace the toner and begin printing. I go to the restroom to wash my hands. AND WE'RE OFF!!! The OCD begins with a powerful thought that I am covered in toner dust. It is on my clothes, my hands, in my mouth, my hair, the floor, my desk, etc. It's everywhere. The truth is that I just changed a printer toner and my hand slightly touched the toner reel. I washed my hands for a while with soap. I left the bathroom. So, to recap, I had a thought and a cleanliness issue from the toner. I walked out of the bathroom and my friends were waiting for me as we had a standing lunch date. I met the lunch crowd and we left the office. The toner thought grew to the point that I felt that I was going to eat my lunch covered in toner. So, needless to say, I would ingest it and basically be eating poison. I knew the reality which is that it is impossible and I washed my hands heavily with soap. The reality does not matter to the OCD. I did have the help of the Zoloft. Needless to say, I just blew it off by thinking "So I'll be eating toner. It will add flavor to my lunch." It took a few minutes, but the thought and anxiety lowered and lowered. Half way through lunch it was over. I ended up enjoying my lunch with my work friends.

After lunch, there were tons of new thoughts, feelings and anxiety to deal with. I had the usual office thoughts such as, "Did I save the file correctly?" "Did I screw the contract database up?", "Did I send out the right invoices with the correct amounts?". I had the oldie but goodie, "Did I spell the person's name correctly that I was emailing." This happens even after you've emailed the same person over and over for years. It's a fun one.

Well, it's now 5:45 on a Friday night. I begin to fill out my time card. I fill in the hours that I worked for each day of the week. I immediately get a thought that I was filling in the incorrect time. This would mean that I lied to the company with a fraudulent time card. They will pay me for my time and, since it is a lie, I am basically stealing from the company. I sit with the thought. Due to the Zoloft, it ended rather quickly. I knew the reality was that my time card was correct and there was no fraud. My boss came into my office and asked about the status of a project. I discussed it and asked what the next step would be. He added a few new requirements. Since it was Friday night, I asked if these new requirements could be done on Monday or did he need it done right away. This would mean that I would work late that night and come in on the weekend. He said "Monday is fine." I immediately got a thought of doubt. "Did he say that Monday is fine?" or "Did he say they needed it immediately and that I should work late to complete it?". I felt that I should repeat with him as to the due date. I quickly add a "Are you sure that Monday is fine?". He responds "Sure, it can wait. The client isn't coming in until Thursday. Take your time". I said "Okay." I'm sure you know me by now. It was NOT okay. The anxiety began. I felt that I should work late to make sure. I was filled with doubt and fear that I would screw this project up. All of a sudden, I got a beep on my computer. It was an email from my boss. The email said that he received the invoices we were waiting for and that I should have a good weekend. The thought and anxiety still persisted. The compulsion was to open the email and read it a certain number of sets to make sure that I can confirm that the project can be done on Monday. I started doing the compulsion by reading over and over "Have a great weekend.". Then I would repeat to myself. "No working this weekend. The project can be done on Monday!" I did it a few times. It is now 6:45pm. I then just said "Let the Zoloft work!". I got up from my desk, turned in my time card and left the office. I made it through another week of working with OCD.

I just want to take a minute to address the fact that each one of the above thoughts take time, effort and strength to fight. They all have their own compulsions to do. They may seem like just a few paragraphs in a book, but I assure you, there are ten times more thoughts, feelings and anxiety in each and every day. I just wanted to give you a quick idea of how the behavior therapy worked while I was on the Zoloft. Some require a certain number or sets with certain numbers of double checking to equal the "Right" number of times. Remember, it becomes about the numbers and compulsions without anything to do with the actual check to see if someone's name is spelled correctly. It's all about how many times you checked it. That's how the system works. On any given day, someone with OCD can have ten times more thoughts. There are many times that thoughts overlap and you have to make sure that you do the right compulsions for the right thoughts. If each thought lasts one hour or more, it can take ten hours out of your daily life. Remember, I just wanted to go to work, do my job and leave like everybody else in the world. I also want to remind you that I left out many thoughts due to time. I would love to tell you that this is all I have to deal with. It is not. I spend hours and hours on the OCD maintenance. I described a little of my work day. Don't forget that there is the time before work and after. It's basically every waking moment. I just mentioned the time in the office while I was trying to work. I just tried to give you a quick idea of what it is like using the behavior therapy while on the Zoloft.

If I explained each and every thought, this book would be 1000 pages. Anyway, I had finally left work. I was meeting a friend for dinner. At this point, I needed some social activity. As usual, I brought my OCD with me.

I went into the office parking structure while doing my usual after work repeating. Going over the day's work while repeating that I got everything done. Due to the Zoloft, the anxiety and thoughts were much lower. I finally said "I'm not doing it! I said it! I am not repeating!" The thoughts and anxiety quickly went away. I drove to dinner. I was on the golden 250 milligrams of Zoloft.   So, when I parked, I just used the behavior therapy and walked away. The anxiety was low enough to ignore any thought of locking the car. I was able to just blow it off and not do it. The thought and feeling was still there. I simply said "Who gives a damn!", "So the car will be stolen!", "That's why I have insurance!". I kept walking. The thought lightened a little as did the anxiety. Little by little it faded away. All of a sudden, the thought, feeling and anxiety are completely gone or so low that it did not even distract me. What used to take hours without medication only took a few minutes. The thought of "Should I just do it?" is plain and simply "Nope!" I was relaxed and calm and able to move on to a great dinner. It was terrific and quiet in my head. My friend and I had a great time with some great conversation.

The overall bottom line with the combination of behavior therapy and medication is that you need both. The behavior therapy began to work when I started on the Zoloft, but not before. I was smashing every thought, feeling, number and set that the OCD threw at me. The thoughts, feelings and anxiety went away much faster. A thought that used to consume me and take hours or days to go away was over in a matter of minutes. There were actually less and less thoughts. There was a lot less times the anxiety was even attached. It was a longer and longer calm space in between each time I had a thought, a feeling or any OCD whatsoever. A subject matter that I could not mention in fear of setting off the OCD and having to deal with it, soon became a subject I was able to discuss. It was a major shift in power. I did what I wanted, when and how. Nothing could stop me. I was able to break out of the OCD box and live my life. I actually became bored during the day due to all the free time I had without the checking, counting, repeating, etc. I felt that I had tons of free time. I enjoyed the newly found freedom. I was in complete control of the OCD for the first time in my life and loved every minute of it.

As for the emotional side, it was AWESOME! I felt strong and powerful for the first time. Remember, the OCD is like a bully or a spoiled little child that does not get the candy that he or she wants in the market. We've all seen, and some of us have been, the parents of a screaming child in a supermarket. The kid is in the aisle, screaming and crying his or her eyes out. Yelling and making noise. Maybe laying on the floor refusing to get up and move on. The point is to DEMAND ATTENTION!!! and get what he or she wants. Imagine how great it would be if you could just walk away from the kid, ignore the screams, don't care about the fit, do not take any time dealing with the child. Imagine there was no time begging, pleading, bargaining or trying to reach any common ground whatsoever. You have the power and the control. Let's take it further and let me ask you this: "What if the child stopped having the fit in the middle of the aisle in the supermarket while you're in public trying to get things done?" A second question: What if you did things without any regard as to whether there will be a fit or not? Question three: What if these fits stopped faster and faster and happened less and less because you gave them no credence? As any parent reading this would know, that sounds pretty great. Am I right? Well, to someone with OCD, that's what the combination of medication and behavior therapy is like. That's what it feels like. That's how much life you would get back.

There are many other emotional changes that occur. I felt very confident and strong. This comes from never having to worry about touching something, saying something or doing something that would trigger OCD. The result is that I did not fear doing things. I did not avoid doing things. I did not fear living my life. I had confidence at work. I did not worry about screwing up or making a mistake. The reality of life sets in. Basically, anything I screwed up can be simply fixed and ended immediately. I was not afraid to be at fault. I admitted when I was wrong to whichever boss with no fear of retribution. I simply fixed the problem and apologized for being wrong. Everybody was very receptive and I ended up getting positive feedback. This gave me confidence to go to work and I did not live in fear of my own mistakes. I did not spend any time counting, checking, repeating, thinking should I or should I not do the compulsions, I had no anxiety, I had very few thoughts, etc. The result was that I got my work done much easier, quicker and with less mistakes. It was amazing! I was getting more and more work done with ease. I felt terrific. The sadness and fear of life was gone. This made me engage in life more, talk to people more and use my sense of humor more. I did not worry if I made a bad joke, insulted someone or was accidentally mean to someone. I did not worry about being rude. It also helped that I was not afraid of people even if they themselves were mean and rude. I was able to deal with them with complete and utter ease. My life became worthwhile. Without being under the control of the OCD, I did not have depression. Yes, I know the anti-depressants in the Zoloft were in full working order. I do know that I was becoming less depressed without the OCD. Not having to battle the OCD made the difference. This was fantastic. I could live like this for the rest of my life. Phew, I was safe now and done living like that.

Well, not so fast. Let's jump ahead six months. If you remember, I lived in Los Angeles and my Sister lived in the San Francisco Bay Area. She had her first child. I was upped in title to an Uncle. "Uncle Jeff". Sounds good, right? I was excited. I wanted to move up to the Bay Area and be part of my nephew's life and for him to be part of mine. I decided I would make the move up to Northern California. With my new found freedom, I had the energy to create a job and the move to the Bay Area. I will not bother you with the boring details of my packing. We all know what moving is like. It is a heinous experience.

Let's jump ahead. I am now living in the Bay Area. I go to fill my next Zoloft prescription. This is the first prescription that I have filled in the Bay Area. I brought my empty bottle into the local pharmacy and the pharmacist came out to the counter and said that this medication has a cap of 200 milligrams. I explained to him that my Doctor in L.A. had been prescribing the 250 for months. He said that he cannot do it. The cap is 200 milligrams and nothing more. It was late and I was tired of unpacking all day. I just said fine. I figured that since the behavior therapy was working so well that nothing can change that. I will NEVER go back to living like I did with the OCD. That's over for me. After all, it's only 50 milligrams, right? What's the worst that can happen? Famous last words.

A few weeks went by and I started to notice a little difference. The OCD was a little stronger and slightly harder to contain. The behavior therapy worked, but not as good as it did before. After a while, I started to get nervous. Is the medication failing? Is it not working? Does it wear off? I reviewed my current life and I was not under any more stress than usual.

I continued to use the behavior therapy. The thoughts and feelings slightly increased more and more over the next few months. I started doing the compulsions again. I needed more relief. I figured that if I found a doctor that was able to help me by putting my prescription back to 250 milligrams, I would be back in business.

I remember the Doctors in L.A. that started me on the Zoloft also mentioned that if you increase the dose and then lower it; it is never as strong as it was. The example of this is that if you are on 200 milligrams and go back down to 150 milligrams, then go back up to 200 milligrams, it will never be as strong as it was the first time you were up to 200 milligrams. So, basically, when I went down from 250 milligrams to 200 milligrams, the entire potency of the Zoloft got screwed.

I found a Doctor who helped me. I received the 250 Milligram prescription. I filled it and went back to my life. I was still overweight and had symptoms return. Nice huh? The 250 milligrams certainly did not work the way that it did before. The Zoloft was no longer working as it used to. It was harder and harder to use the behavior therapy.

A few more months went by. I was back getting the thoughts and anxiety. I was also back doing the compulsions. There was more bad news as I was overweight, losing my hair and very tired all of the time. Great situation, right? I felt that I was back where I started without the Zoloft.

I had an idea. I went from 150 to 200 to 250 and felt increasingly better at each level. Logic would dictate that if I went to 300, then I would feel that much better. It also would give the behavior therapy the jump start that it needed. Needless to say, it was back to the Doctor for me. The doctor was skeptical as the 300 was 100 milligrams over the recommended limit of 200. He decided to give it a try. I received the 300 milligram prescription and went on my way.

I was now on 300 milligrams of Zoloft. It was a very strong anti-depressant with the least amount of side effects. Although, I would consider balding, overweight and tiredness a side effect. Wouldn't you? I was on the most medication that I've ever been on. Anyway, a few months went by and there was no change in the OCD. The thoughts and anxiety were right there with me as they always were. There was no ease and no hopes of the behavior therapy working. I still had hopes for the Zoloft to work.

Are you ready for more bad news? My insurance company stopped covering the brand name version of the medication. Up to now, I'd only been on the brand name Zoloft. The brand name is the first kind of the medication. It is the real version. It is produced by the actual pharmaceutical company that invented it. They file for a patent that lasts many years. Eventually, the patent runs out. This means that any company on earth can now start to produce their version of the medication with a similar formula. This is known as a "Generic" drug. As you know, they are much cheaper than the original or brand name. The insurance companies love the generic versions of medications as they are cheap. This is why they cover a lot of them as their side of the co-pay is MUCH less than with the brand name. I know that's more than you ever needed or wanted to know about the pharmaceutical industry. The Doctor who took a chance and increased the Zoloft to 300 milligrams told me that there was a 25 percent difference in strength between the brand and the generic version of medications. I have no idea if this is true or not. It was enough to scare me into seeking out the brand name.

I began to research how I could obtain the brand name. I was on a very strong brain medication. This is why I did not want to mess around and switch to a lower cost version. I discovered that you could order the brand name from another country. Relax, it's perfectly legal. You need to send the prescription to the pharmacy in the country you are ordering from. Once on file, they can send you the brand name and for the Zoloft, it was a much lower price. I did the above and received the brand name of the Zoloft. I was back in business.

It is now a year later. I was ordering the Zoloft from another country. I was still on the 300 milligrams of the brand. It was not really working. The OCD returned and the behavior therapy was useless. I was very depressed. No, the anti-depressants in the Zoloft had no effect. I figured that if I was on 300 milligrams of the brand name, had anxiety, was overweight, was losing my hair, was tired all of the time and STILL had all the OCD; what was the point? I will return to the medication research to look for something better. By now, medical technology has grown so there had to be something better. I met with a neurologist and sure enough Zoloft was still the best on the market with the least amount of side effects. I went online and researched the new medications on the market. They were all filled with horrible side effects that were worse than the OCD itself.

I thought about it for a few days. I realized that I should try getting off the Zoloft completely. I could not just go cold turkey with a strong pharmaceutical that I had been on for so many years. I went down little by little. After I was off of the medication for a few weeks, I did notice a difference. There was more anxiety and the thoughts were stronger. I felt feelings that I have not felt in a long time. I was also very depressed. A few weeks went by and I decided that the Zoloft did actually help. Not with the OCD or the behavior therapy. The help was with the anxiety. It did not help a lot, but even the slightest amount is better than nothing. So, needless to say. I went back on the generic version known as Sertraline (Zoloft). I figured that if I was still going to have the OCD and would only be taking it for a slight edge on the anxiety, I would rather pay 10 dollars per month than the few hundred I was paying for years. I went back to knowing that it was not a quick fix and would not make the behavior therapy work. I figured that even a small kick with the anxiety is all I'm going to get and that was better than nothing.

I was now up to 150 milligrams of the generic version. After a few years, I decided to lower the medication as low as I can. The least amount of chemicals in the body the better. I was able to go down to 50 milligrams. If either way, my freedom was gone. Why have a lot of medication in my system? Why bother. It's not going to change, right?

The overall reality with the medication game is that it can be a rough life. I was on the Zoloft raising and lowering the dosage for eleven plus years. The thing that I've learned is that it does not fully work. It makes you feel better and stronger when you first start it. Then, your body gets used to it and that's it. The neurologists, pharmaceutical companies and the medical community don't really care if you get better as they want a customer for life. They would be very happy if you suffer enough to take the medication for life whether it helps you or not. The doctors and scientists inventing these medications don't know what it is like to live with OCD so they cannot really fix it. They just do some focus group research and try a bunch of things. They find something that makes one group happy and its time to bring the drug to mass market. They have the added bonus of hoping your health care plan covers it for life. You will worry that it will be taken off the market. You will be nervous that you will forget it on a vacation. You will need to mess with the dosage, see doctors for a prescription, go through the blood tests, etc. If you move to another city, you will need to find new doctors to fill the prescriptions. Don't forget about the emotional issues with the fact that you are taking a medication for the OCD and still have it. They all have side effects. There might be dizziness, carbohydrate cravings, sleep issues, overweight, hair loss, etc. Great that an anti-depressant causes these depressing side effects. What the hell kind of joke is that?

The bottom line is that all of the medications on the market do not help fix or cure the OCD. They just numb it and try to cover up the problem. The put you in an altered state where you "Feel" less pain. You are not actually out of pain. Just like a standard pain killer. They just mask the problem. They do not fix it. The most you will get from the medication is a little help with the anxiety and nothing else. But hey, free side effects! Yeah! The second you come off of it or lower the dose, everything returns. The people that make these medications target one major issue: The fact THAT you have OCD! They do not know or care WHY you have OCD! What really causes it! What is the actual reason that you have OCD! The point is why bother to take something that is so fragile that one difference in dosage and all is ruined. I started out with OCD and have been on the Zoloft for nineteen years. I still have OCD.

CHAPTER 14: HOMEOPATHIC/ NATURAL MEDICATIONS!

"I Tried Some Pot To Get Rid Of My Irrational Thought!"

I have discussed pharmaceutical medications such as my Zoloft in the previous chapter. This chapter is about the opposite side of the medical community. The homeopathic or all natural medications. These are simply the medications that are designed and created by companies that are the opposition for the big pharmaceutical companies. The pharmaceutical companies or "Big Pharma" is a multibillion dollar industry. This industry designs and creates chemical medications with side effects. They produce a product if there is a need for it. They have billion-dollar lab facilities. They hire the best of the best from the top schools. They have chemists, biologists, scientists, doctors, miscellaneous medical professionals, investors, as well as the contracts to distribute their new products. Some of the products really work and others fail. The point is that these companies are huge and produce medications with side effects that need attention from more medications. If they can relieve someone's pain, it is a success. If one of their medications doesn't work; there are many others to choose from. They manufacture their products in labs. Their products are all chemically based and therefore synthetic. They might help someone and they might not. There can be excellent effects and results from their products. There can also be tons and tons of side effects. We have all seen the commercials trying to sell their products.

The commercial will have someone with allergies or another problem. The first half of the commercial will show a person breathing freely in a field of beautiful flowers while enjoying their life and playing with an adorable giggling baby. The second half of the commercial will mention all of the possible side effects. The same woman who was breathing and playing with the new baby might have all sorts of complications from the medication. They go on and on. They mention that you should discontinue their product if any of these symptoms occur. So by the end of the wonderful commercial that is designed to sell their product, you end up disgusted. You soon realize that the woman you are watching giggling with the baby in a field may have the side effects. She can breathe right but at what cost.

Anyway, you get the idea. The chemicals are dangerous and cause major side effects that are often worse than the initial reason for taking the medication in the first place. Most of the time, these chemicals, such as pain killers, just mask the problem. They just cover the pain without actually addressing the root cause. That is why you need to take them for a while and every four to six hours. They know that once they wear off, the pain will come right back. They are not fixing anything. They are just covering it. And unfortunately some of these painkillers are addictive.

Having said that, there are many people that wanted to develop healthy products that actually work with the body. This type of thinking spawned the homeopathic industry. This industry functions exactly like the chemical based industry. They have the same chemists, doctors, scientists, etc. The difference is that these companies try to manufacture an alternative to the chemical version of a medication. These products might be all natural or organic supplements. They might be plant based, animal based or a lab compounded creation. The point of this industry is to come up with healthy solutions to the big pharmaceutical companies. The overall point of their medications is that the least amount of chemicals is the best. They make the casings for the capsules, the liquids if needed, the tablets, etc.

They get their ideas from all over the world. A lot of them might come from the eastern style of medicine. The western side is known for its chemical base. The eastern style is usually more natural and organic. The eastern doctors use the same products that have been used for thousands of years. Some have a proven track record of success with millions of people. The homeopathic companies are trying to manufacture something with less or no side effects. Their goal is something that is not synthetic. They shoot for something that is natural and safe for human consumption with the same effects as the strong processed chemicals that the huge pharmaceutical companies are mass producing.

The problem or main obstacle of this health focused industry is that the laws are different for them. The FDA does not track or regulate them. This means that investment possibilities are limited. There is then limited money in their budget for control group testing, focus groups, journals, studies, published lab findings, validated results. There are no generic versions, no insurance company coverage or co-pay assistance. There are no giant insurance companies with contracts to push their products. No doctors will use their products in their practice. The pharmaceutical company representatives will not handle them. The major pharmacy chains will not recommend them. This has a dramatic effect on their industry.

They are limited in their capabilities. The problem with this is that someone who wants to try one of their products might have a lot of trouble trying to research their medications. Their labels are clear as to what is in them but you would try it at your own risk. Maybe it works and maybe it does not.

Most people would not even consider a cheap alternative or something not needing a prescription. Most people would think that they would pale in comparison to anything that a real pharmaceutical company can offer to the masses. With OCD, there is always a "Hope" theory. This theory is based on the hope that one of these companies will come up with or invent something that will bring sweet relief from the OCD. Something that will free us from this constant suffering. We live with the hope that there will someday be a cure where we can live our lives without this constant pain from living in a system of numbers and worthless thoughts that are combined with pointless compulsions. Something that we can either take alone as a main drug or as an addition to a pharmaceutical. Guess what, I am no different. Over the past twenty-five years or so, I have tried a few of these so called treatments. Let me tell you about some of them.

I want to first mention that when you go to various doctors or therapists, you end up with many different opinions. You have to start fresh with each doctor. Each doctor gives you their song and dance as to what you need and how they can help you. Each doctor gives you a completely different opinion. They all contradict each other. So, right away, you are not sure who is right. Who do you listen to? You start fresh with each doctor and they start you off on what they think is the correct way to help you. They all think that their methods are the best. They all believe that they are correct. You are left to do your own online research. You get to a point where you wonder what you are paying them for. Anyway, they each take time to try their methods. You always hope that you have finally found the right person who will actually help you. Unfortunately, this is not always the case. You end up spending a lot of time, money and effort. This usually ends with you leaving them in search of better relief. Basically, you have just spent a big waste of time on someone who was wrong. It is unfortunate and a shame. The reality is that with OCD, you need to waste this time and hope for the best. After all, you may actually hit on something that helps you. The reality is that with Obsessive Compulsive Disorder, you will continue to try and find a "cure". It is a regular pursuit for the cure that is out there and needs to be found.

There are many different forms that these homeopathic

remedies can come in. They come in pills, tablets, powders, gels, liquids, weird gummy type items, acupuncture, aromatherapy, teas, etc.. Since these medications are not actual pharmaceuticals, they are very weak. Most of which need a high dose or consumption in order to work. The problem with this is that you are also ingesting large amounts of the product. If they use a special coating or some other thing to enhance the consumption, you are eating and digesting it. It does not always mean that this will work for you.

I have tried a lot of these different supplements and body techniques. Each one is named with something to do with what it is trying to fix. They might also be named after something like the effect that they are designed to create. They might be named nerves-be-gone, anxiety free, calm down, easy does it, relax-o-pill, thoughts be gone, number go away, clear head, etc. Each name is unique and created by the company that made it. These names try to give you an idea as to what they can do. The truth is that, if you do not need a prescription for it, chances are it is not too strong. If they sell it right near the M & M's, then that should tell you that they work on the OCD just as well as the M & M's would. If they sell them next to the booze, then that tells you that the booze is a better choice to battle the OCD. Just kidding!

I have tried a few different types of these homeopathic/natural drugs. Sometimes they are called nutraceuticals. Nutraceuticals have a few different doses depending on what they contain. There are some that you will need to just take one pill. There are some that you will need to take a lot of pills at various times of the day. Some of the doses are "As Needed". It depends on what the medication is made up of and what form the medication is in. These nutraceuticals come in many forms. They can be a liquid, a powder, something that you suck on or chew on or a simple pill. They can be in many different forms due to the fact that they are not a typical pharmaceutical which has rules and regulations as to how it is made.

The doses are usually once a day or multiple times each

day. Sometimes they are taken in the morning and sometimes they are taken at night. There are some that you just take throughout the day. There are even a few that you only take at the first onset of an OCD issue. The problem with these is that, by then, it is way too late. Once the OCD starts, it started...period. No little hippie leaf will stop it or help whatsoever.

Let's walk through a few of the things that I have tried. It was a long and drawn out process that took me years to complete. I have tried many different things. Some of them had a small effect at first. But, then the symptoms came right back. Some things worked but did not work enough to validate taking it or the expense of the procedure. Some of the things did not work at all. Either way, it was an experience to try each and every one of these things.

The first thing that I tried was when the explosion hit when I was twenty-two. I was in the middle of horrible OCD. I tried something called Kava Kava Root. It was supposed to induce a calm and relaxed state. It was supposed to calm me down. It was designed to promote relaxation. Needless to say, NOPE! It did not have any effects whatsoever on the OCD. Imagine that a liquid made from a plant or whatever could not cure my OCD. Are you as surprised as I am?

I tried a tea made out of wood bark. That's right. You read that correctly. It was a tea made out of tree bark. There were pieces of branches, leaves, twigs, etc. Not exactly English breakfast tea. It smelled just as bad as you can imagine. It smelled like dirty garbage that was flavored with an old sock. I had to drink it cold a few times a day. It felt like I just went into my backyard and grabbed a handful of sticks and dirt, cooked them and started drinking it. It was a horrible nasty experience. Needless to say NOTHING CHANGED!

I tried acupuncture. I figured that since the wood tea did not work, maybe I would try some needles to the face. It was my first time so I did not know what to expect. They start off by telling you what the needles do and the different parts of the body that they put the needles in and why. They basically explain why they need to stab you in the brain. I laid on the table and a doctor put needles in my chest, face and feet. He then left the room. I thought to myself, "Great! This is exactly what I need to calm myself down!" "Why didn't I think of that?" "Laying in a bed with needles to the face." I laid there for about half an hour. The results were absolutely nothing. Not a damn thing changed with the OCD. It was another worthless attempt.

I tried a powder called Inositol. It is basically a powder in a bottle. The way it is taken is to mix it with a liquid. You drink this powdery crap and it is supposed to help you to relax. It is one of the "Take as needed" type thing. It was one of the things that you need to take an awful lot of throughout the day. It was ridiculous. It did not help at all.

There is also something called 5HTP. It is a pill type thing that is supposed to cause a relaxed state. It is most likely used as an ingredient in some of these, so called, nutraceuticals. I tried it with absolutely no change whatsoever.

There was a serotonin pill that was supposed to create serotonin in my brain. I felt a difference the first few days that I took it. Then, as per usual, it went south and nothing changed within the world of OCD. SURPRISE! It did not work.

I took what looked like a Lego piece. It was a sort of square piece that was rectangle and had bumps on the top of it. It might as well have been a Lego piece. I needed to swallow it and it was supposed to calm me down. Yet again, nothing.

Yes, I tried pot. That is to say the legal kind. I tried CBD oil. I went to my local distillery. I told the guy at the counter that I had OCD. I asked for a recommendation. I don't think he had any idea of what to do or what OCD even stood for. But, he tried. He told me that a Sativa base would be a great place to start. I made my purchase and went on my way. I went home and tried it. I took the dose which was half an eyedropper full. I put it under my tongue and let it absorb. A few minutes later, I started to feel the effects. Remember, this product has extremely low THC so the effects are limited. I am not getting stoned or high. I simple got a little relaxed. I noticed the effects. I needed to get used to it as it might get stronger the more I take it. I tried it a few times. It just gave me the numbing effect. There was absolutely no change within the OCD. I still had thoughts and the feeling to do the compulsions. This told me that CBD will not have a desired effect on the OCD. Hey, at least I tried. It was another failure.

My overall critique of these alternative medicinal products is that they do not work for me. They are usually sold in that weird section of a natural foods market. They are usually not regulated by anyone. They are made by companies that no one has ever heard of. They offer a wide variety of solutions for everything that you need. The only problem is that they are not a pharmaceutical. This means that they are not strong. They are not actual chemicals like real medications. They are not researched as well as they should be. They are not manufactured in a high power lab. A pharmaceutical takes years to produce and there are trials and trials prior to its release. The government watches these companies like a hawk. The homeopathic and natural supplement industry is far weaker and does not have the money to support its products.

They all use products that are made from some sort of juice extract, outdoor leaf, animal, tree, etc. They are usually invented by people who know about medicinal cures but hate the pharmaceutical empire. They are trying to develop something with the least amount of dangerous side effects and I understand this. But in my experience, they do not produce anything with a result whatsoever.

These medications are made by people that think that natural products can cure someone. They are all into a natural way of life. They all feel that they need to live off of the land. They do research and find out that a tree in Costa Rica may cure cancer. The reality is that trees, flowers, animals and berries do not really have a cure for anything like OCD. There is no cure whatsoever even though the people I met with believed there was. Needless to say, nothing I tried worked at all and had a short lifespan. They were all worthless. They all did not create a change in the OCD at all.

In conclusion, I have tried many different things. I have tried a lot of different homeopathic and natural or nutraceutical products. I started off the same with each of them. I started off hopeful that there might be a desired result. I hoped that there was a cure or that I would, at least, feel some relief from the Obsessive Compulsive Disorder. Time and time again, I was let down. These products just did not work. They were all a letdown and ended up having no effect on the OCD. These products might be good for some people, but they do nothing for someone with OCD. I really tried in hopes to get some relief from my symptoms. The truth is that there is a reason that these natural remedies do not have a multi-billion-dollar industry attached to them. They just do not work like a pharmaceutical. In truth, I have a lot of respect for the concept of homeopathy and I hope it is in fact helping many people with lesser problems than I have.

CHAPTER 15: OVERALL WELLNESS!

"Better Late Zen Never!"

I have discussed the different medical treatments that I have tried. I mentioned the pharmaceutical medications as well as the homeopathic or natural medications. There is one other type of "Medication". That is the overall wellness of a human being. This overall wellness is a large part of everyday life. Everyone strives for some form of wellness in their daily lives. It can be a very important component in who we are as people. We all have our own versions of wellness. We all have different feelings as to what wellness is and how to achieve it.

As you can imagine, having OCD will have an effect on your overall wellness plan. We have all read the online articles on the various wellness sites. There are many different people that you can discuss this with. You can ask your doctor, therapist or even your yoga instructor. There are many people that will tell you what the true meaning of wellness is. They will go on and on about their personal theory. They will tell you about the different things that they do in a day. They might even bring up the fact that it might just be a state of mind. The truth of the matter is that it is really up to you to seek out what theories and practices that you feel bring total wellness into your life.

You can talk to many different people and get into a long discussion. If you talk to a karate instructor, they might say that the strength from mastering their martial art is true power. If you talk to a yoga instructor, they might tell you that their practice gives them true happiness. If you speak to a Priest or a Rabbi, they will tell you that your faith is the key. If you talk to a farmer, they might tell you to get lost and get off of their land. Hey, it might happen. The point is that you can talk to anyone and will get a completely different answer. They will all contradict each other. They will all tell you what works for them. Their answer does not mean in any way, shape or form that they know what will work for you. While talking to them, or if they know you, the subject of OCD might come up. This will usually change a little of what they are talking about. They will tell you that they know what you need. They will tell you that they will help you. The conversation will usually start off with "Here's what you need to do." This is coincidentally the exact moment that I stop listening. Everyone has an answer. Everyone knows what it right. Everyone has a cure for OCD. Once again, the people you are asking do not have OCD. This changes a lot. They might know what works for someone without OCD. They might know how to calm themselves down. But for you, it just might be some worthless information. Not to be mean, but it most likely will not work for you or your OCD. So, basically, try at your own risk. It might calm you down, but that does not mean that it will have any possible effect on your OCD.

The realistic answer consists of more than one thing. You will need to be the best version of yourself that you can. This means that you need to work on the entire package. Not just one aspect. The reality is that you will need to incorporate all facets of life. This will include the usual diet and exercise and relaxing items. This will include inner and outer exercises. Since I have OCD, I have definitely tried a few of these things in hope of feeling better and maybe, just maybe, lowering the OCD in the process. Let me tell you about some of things that I tried.

The first thing that I tried in terms of wellness is a diet. This began when I was a child. My Mother took me to a doctor who said that sugar was a major cause of the OCD. So needless to say, like any concerned Mother, she changed her shopping habits. She made some different choices when doing the weekly shopping. She stocked the house with low sugar sodas. This was in hopes that the less sugar that I have, the less OCD I will have. She also chose better things in the snack department. We were the house that had safe and low fat snacks. We had low salt pretzels, low sugar candy, snacks with healthy choices. My Mother cooked a low fat dinner every night. We had a safe refrigerator. My Mother did not buy a lot of things that were highly processed. The lower the food dyes or additives, the better. She bought the healthiest foods available at the time.

The other aspect that was mentioned by a doctor was physical activity. Now, this was a long time ago so kids actually had to leave their house to have fun. So, physical activity was not a problem. The other thing that happened was that my Mother signed me up for karate lessons at a local Dojo. She figured that this would insure that enough exercise was being completed on a weekly basis.

As I got older, okay, okay, much older, my weight was being affected by my horrible eating habits as well as the Zoloft. These medications tend to put weight on. In some cases, it can be a lot of weight. So, as you may have guessed, it was back to diet. This was a different diet. It was based off of the premise that I would feel better if I eat better. The "You are what you eat" theory. The overall diet was designed to lose weight. I was told that the lower the weight, the better I will feel about my life. I will also have less fat on the brain. I agreed to it due to the fact that the Zoloft deals with overall body chemistry. The thought was that the lower the fat my body has, the less fat the Zoloft will have to get through, the stronger the Zoloft will be. So, I took on the challenge. I hired a trainer and changed my eating habits.

I bought grass fed organic beef. I did not buy any snacks. I cut out soda. I tried to stay away from all greasy foods that are high in fat. I was trained to fear carbs. I stayed away from everything good like cheese, bacon, breads, salty snacks, chocolates, processed foods etc. I ate home most of the time. I tried to eat the best that I could. I bought organic meats, fruits, vegetables and groceries.

I started to work out as much as possible. I tried to work out regularly. I made it my purpose to always make time for some form of exercise. I did muscle stuff and cardio with my trainer. It was hard work. It was also expensive. I worked with the trainer for six months.

Let me sum up the diet and exercise theory. The good news is that the diet and exercise was excellent and I ended up losing weight. The bad news is that I was told by a holistic doctor that this would work. His point was that the better I eat, the better I will feel. The OCD might lower. SURPRISE!!! No change in the OCD whatsoever. I actually had repeating, counting and lingering thoughts while I was busting my ass with the trainer. So, the first thing I realized is that diet does not have any effect on the OCD. The second thing that I learned is that the vigorous insane nonstop physical exercise did NOT have ANY effect on the OCD. I was spending 45 minutes working out with a professional. Each workout had a huge portion of weight lifting and cardio. It was very difficult. I had thoughts, feelings, repeating and lingering thoughts. They happened before, during and after each session. The point being that the OCD still was strong during the fitness sessions. This tells me that the OCD will not stop even during prime moments of very difficult exercise. The holistic doctor had told me that diet and exercise would help with the OCD. It really had no effect on the Obsessive Compulsive Disorder whatsoever. Not even a little. I was at the gym one day and had a lingering thought on the treadmill. I had anxiety on the treadmill. I have done repeating on the treadmill.

I also learned that no amount of high protein or low fat diet would work. Basically, the doctor that told me that it would; did not know a thing about what he was talking about. Diet and exercise was not the answer for OCD. Eating organic pesticide free broccoli will not get rid of an irrational thought. Steel cut oatmeal will not get rid of the anxiety and a fresh fruit will not stop the compulsions.

I even tried to change the way that I ate. I put myself on a schedule where I ate three meals a day. Maybe the metabolism will affect something. I tried it with no results whatsoever. The results were that I did eventually lose weight. I did feel better about myself. I did look better. Guess what? The OCD was just as bad as when I was overweight and eating fattening food. The theory that the less fat on the brain would lower the OCD had no credence. The fact that the Zoloft works with body chemistry and would become stronger as it has less fat to get through was also a complete fairy tale. Hey, at least I lost some weight and put on some muscle through that research.

I went to another so called wellness expert. This doctor told me that the Obsessive Compulsive Disorder was energy based. The best way to get rid of or help the OCD was to blow out that energy with quick and vigorous exercise. He suggested jumping rope. I figured that it was worth a try. I bought a jump rope. There I was sitting in my apartment waiting for the OCD to trigger so I could test the theory. As you can guess, it did. I stood up with excitement and jumped rope. I did it for a few minutes until I was exhausted. The OCD was right there with me. The thought and feeling to repeat stayed right where it was. The OCD did not give a crap that I was jumping rope. The point of the quick and fast paced extreme exercise was to "Blow Out" the extra energy to get rid of the thought, anxiety and compulsion. This did not work at all. I am sort of glad as it would have made life odd. I would have had to bring a jump rope with me everywhere I went. I would have been on a date in a nice restaurant and had to tell my date to please excuse me. Then, stand up in the restaurant right next to the table and jump rope for a few minutes until the server was done putting out the salads. Then, I would sit back down like nothing happened and say "So, you were saying." That would have sucked. What kind of life would that have been? I would have had to jump rope like a lunatic in the middle of a store. Someone would have called the police if I started to jump rope like a whacko in a bakery. You see what I mean? I was told that it would work by getting rid of the energy and in turn lowering the OCD. Baloney, Baloney and, what else, oh right, Baloney. That was the second time I was given information from a wellness expert and it was so very wrong. I was forced to conclude that any form of diet and exercise is DEFIN-ITELY not a cure for Obsessive Compulsive Disorder but is in fact a part of wellness.

The next thing that I tried was Yoga and Meditation. It was recommended to me that I try both. The thought being to relax you into a calm state by connecting your mind and your body. The yoga and meditation practice would help to put me in a Zen state and calm my brain down. I would not have the OCD or, at least, it would be lower. The key to the OCD was slow down and calm down. This calm energy would lower or get rid of the anxiety. I would be so calm that the OCD would not occur. The thoughts would just flow out of my head. I would not care or want to do the compulsions. The feelings to do things would be calm. I figured, why not, it can't hurt. If it does not work, it would just be another hopeful try.

I found a nearby yoga studio. I signed up for a few classes and began practicing yoga. I brought my yoga mat and bottled water. I was ready to go. I started sitting in the lotus position. The instructor taught us how to do the yoga breathing. You need to learn to breathe slow and controlled in deep spurts. She showed us how to do a few poses or asanas. Poses are when you stand and lean in certain ways to put your body in an ancient position. These positions are all named things like Warrior Pose, Tree Pose, Downward Dog Pose or Tush Pose. Ok, that last one might not be real.

I was in the class doing all the poses. Some successfully and others not so much. It was difficult at first, but got easier as time went on. For those of you that have taken yoga, yes, I did need the foam yoga blocks to complete some of the more flexible positions.

There I was, taking regular yoga classes. I was doing my poses and my breathing. I was able to relax in the classes. There was, however, one big problem. The OCD was horrible all the way up into the classes. Then, continued right after the classes ended. So basically, at most, I was sort of calm for forty-five minutes a day for the three classes a week. Both before and after the classes, I lived in OCD land. This was not such a big help. My feelings were that I suffered tremendously prior to the classes. The second the class ended, I would begin to tremendously suffer. So, what was the point? This was not going to help me in my life whatsoever. I have to be able to live. Was I supposed to move into and live my entire life in an ashram? Clearly this was not going to work for me. I stopped the yoga classes. So much for trying to namaste the crap out of the Obsessive Compulsive Disorder. I chalked it up to another failed attempted to rid myself of this disorder.

It was also recommended that I use the yoga breathing techniques when I had a thought, anxiety or felt like I needed to do compulsions. Once again, how ridiculous. So, if I get an obsession or feel anxious, I am supposed to go into a corner and do ancient huffing and puffing until I am calm. Imagine if you were in line at a supermarket and the person behind you started deep breathing in a controlled fashion. After shaking in your pants, you would never go back to that store again. You see the point? Everyone tells you different things which are fine if they do not have to do them. They don't care if you walk around ancient breathing on everyone. How would they feel if they had to live like that? The truth of the matter is that the breathing did not work at all. So, it was more worthless advice from someone without OCD. It was definitely not going to help. Time to move on.

I was simultaneously meditating. The point is that meditation would bring me into a relaxed and Zen type state. It is an ancient practice that would help me become one with myself, get in the zone or some other type of relaxing baloney. I would then be able to calm down the OCD. I tried by sitting into the lotus position and closing my eyes. I calmed down my breathing and sat there for a few minutes. I was told to try and envision a wall. The wall was representing the OCD. I was supposed to envision myself breaking through the wall. I guess a symbolic gesture of breaking through the OCD (The Wall) to freedom. I tried it a few times with absolutely no success. It had no effect on the OCD. The thoughts and feelings were there all day. Another brick wall. (Pun intended.)

I tried traditional therapy. My thought was that this entire OCD storm that has lasted for twenty plus years was due to some emotional issues that I had never dealt with. I figured that it was worth a shot. I did some research and found a therapist. I booked an appointment. I showed up for the appointment. The first thing that I did was fill out pages of information. There were a lot of questions regarding my family background. My first thought was how is my family history is going to help the therapist to decipher what my hidden pain might be now? How does knowing my family history help me today? I decided not to worry about it. I just filled out the stack of paperwork. I was beginning to wonder if I would even get in to see the actual therapist. I continued to fill in my entire family history until I finally got through the mound of paper.

I waited in the waiting room with my newly completed paperwork. A few minutes later, the door opened and she was standing there. I walked in and sat on a couch next to a box of tissues. There are tissues on the table and on a desk. How many tissues am I going to need? What is going to happen in here? Should I worry?

My therapist begins to ask me why I came in. She was very friendly and calming. I mentioned that I have Obsessive Compulsive Disorder. I asked her if she had ever dealt with anyone with this particular disorder. As you can guess, many therapists have worked with people with OCD. It is so common and she knew what my life was like due to it. I asked her if she felt that all of this can be due to some psychological issue that I have? She mentioned that it might be. She wanted to see where it went and what came up.

She asked me lots of questions about my childhood. As you know that is a good place to start. I guess a lot of bad things happens in one's childhood. The funny thing about a person's childhood is that is when we all have the most fun. Most of us are happy and enjoy not having the responsibilities that adulthood brings. Unfortunately, this is also the time that our experiences and emotions dictate how we will view the world. It is a fun and nurturing and important time in one's life. Needless to say, we started discussing my childhood. To tell you the truth, I was kind of hoping for something forgotten in the back of my mind to come out. That way I could just deal with it and move on with my life. I would solve the mystery and end the OCD for life. As you may have guessed, this did not happen.

She kept asking me about my childhood. She discussed my home life as well as my family members. She was interested in how my relationships were with all of the members of my family. We discussed my father, my mother and my sister. I brought up certain things that have happened that were a vivid memory. Some good and some bad. We have all had these good and bad events happen. It is a part of a normal and usual childhood. We discussed these times in my life and found very basic and usual issues. Nothing big or ground breaking. Nothing that would cause or constitute a trauma. We decided to move on.

I told her about the time that I was twenty-two. Since you have already read that chapter, I will not bore you with the details. We discussed the overall events and things that happened to me during that period of my life. We discussed my first breakup. We talked about my mother having been diagnosed with breast cancer. She was lucky and had been able to remove it quickly and go through the healing process. We discussed the stress I was under by going back to college. We even discussed the fact that I was deeply depressed since the OCD exploded on me and had been very bad since then. We discussed the psychological aspects of each of these events that had happened in my life. She went over what people go through during these times. What the pain might be from. Why the depression occurred. She made me realize that I still had pain from these events even though they were a long time ago. There was a lot of fear and anger. We discussed the pain that I went through and how to look at it from an adult perspective.

The therapist explained that there is a part of you that does not grow up. This is your inner child. We all have one. It is a part of you that remains a child. This, I guess is how you can have fun as an adult. Her explanation was that the inner child controlled some aspect of the OCD. The inner child held the OCD in place. This young part of myself kept the OCD going. The idea being that I was afraid of certain aspects of life. This inner child was the part of myself that used the OCD when I was afraid or nervous about something. The OCD might be some sort of coping mechanism.

She would do these exercises where I needed to go into my heart space and connect with my inner child. I would close my eyes and imagine that I was looking at my inner child. I would then give the younger version of myself a huge hug and let him know that he is safe and I will protect him. I did this many times with her. This was completed throughout my therapy sessions. When I was in that state, she would tell me what I needed to tell him. Sometimes I needed to ask him certain things in order to get information from him. This information would let me know what I was secretly afraid of. I would then be able to help myself to understand what was really going on. I would then see what the OCD was actually covering. Then, my therapist and I would get to work on that subject matter to see if we could resolve it. I figured that if this was the case, I would not have the OCD on an issue that has been resolved. So, I gave it a try and went into my heart space. I did this many times over the few years with this particular therapist. I had hoped each and every time that

I would uncover something that would help me to heal and get rid of this awful OCD. But, like everything else in this chapter that I had tried, no luck whatsoever. Speaking with my inner child did not help me with my OCD one bit.

There was another basic issue that I had which was a career. I was not in the place that I wanted to be at that stage of my life. I wanted more out of my career. I did graphic design for many years. Lucky for me, the therapist that I chose was also a life coach. This meant that she also handled and helped people improve their careers. She had a ton of tests and questions for me. These tests were designed to help me see what I was good at. This would eventually lead me to see what careers would be a good fit for me. It would help me decide on a career path that I would excel in. She had recommended a few classes that I should take at the local community college. These classes would do the tests that she felt I should take. She wanted me to bring the test results back to her so she could analyze them. I signed up for the class.

The class was pretty ridiculous. It was a class where you took tests to match your natural abilities to a career. You fill out forms as to what you like to do. There were questions to see what you felt excited about and what you felt comfortable with. Then judge the environment you enjoy most. If you thrive in high stress or low stress environments? Do you like working in teams or on your own? Do you like to be creative or not? Would you prefer to be in a supervisory role or not? I had to answer them all and so I did. I got the results and brought them back to my therapist. They were overall worthless as the results showed that I would be great in marketing or design. That was what I was already doing but with the advent of Photoshop, I was becoming obsolete. So, why did I need to take a class and tests to find out that I am in the career I am best at? It made no sense. They gave ranges of career paths. They might say you would be great at advertising or cleaning toilets. Ok, I made that one up. They gave ranges such as marketing and advertising to sales or legal. The ranges were so ridiculous. The results of the tests did not really help her much. They did nothing for me.

My therapist/life coach took the results and added a few other tests of her own. She asked me what I like and what I think I want to do. What makes me happy. She had a ton of contacts and knew a lot of people and a lot of places for information. She really was able to tell me what my options are. She asked me tons of questions. She made a few suggestions. She felt I would be best at selling coffee in front of office buildings. You know those carts that sell small food items and coffee? I thought, "What the hell?". After the class and answering all of her questions? This is what she came up with? Well that sucks! I quickly realized that she would be no help with career choices at all. I was done.

Some of the things that she had me do were odd. One assignment was to use different color pens on a white piece of large card stock. I was supposed to write my positive traits on the sheet of paper. Each trait needed to be written in a different color. So, basically, I was sitting on her couch thinking that I am spending all of this money to get rid of my OCD. Instead, I am thirty-five years old and coloring like a child. I figured "Screw it" and stopped midway.

She also tried some sort of weird thing that was supposed to help. I believe it was E.M.D.R. or something with letters like that. It was basically a completely insane way of an attempt of a treatment. Here is how it worked. I was supposed to sit on her couch and put these headphones on. Between you and I, they were the cheapest and most uncomfortable headphones ever made. There was a wire coming out of one of the sides of the headphones. The wire was connected to a little box with a switch. My therapist held the box from across the room. She pressed the switch every few seconds. This caused a light clicking sound from the headphones. Every time I heard the clicking, I was supposed to move my eyes from side to side. This was supposed to last a few minutes. The clicking was at a fast pace so I moved my eyes quickly back and forth. Yes, this freak exercise was real. I actually did it. I figured that, "Hey, it might actually work". This eye movement was supposed to help me access a part of my brain. This part might have a memory of hidden trauma. Afterwards, I was supposed to write down all of my memories to see if something comes up. It was also supposed to calm me down. I tried it and it did not work. It was insane to think that if it worked, I would have to keep doing it. I would have to wear these headphones and use them when the OCD kicked up. I would be in the market, near the chips, with cheap headphones while hearing clicking and rapidly moving my eyes back and forth like a lunatic. Gee, is that what people in society want to see? How fast would you run out and never shop at that store again? There are some treatments that you hope do not work. This was one of them. It would be a ridiculous way to live.

I went to this therapist for about two or more years. I did have some very positive results. She really did help me work through some old things that I needed to address. As a whole, the therapy really did help me. I realized a lot about myself. I was able to change a lot and understand even more. I have changed my perspective on a lot of subjects as well as understood my past feelings and why they came to be. I am glad that I went to her. She was a good thing in my life. I changed a lot with her help. The emotional work on my past was a great learning experience. The career work was important. The unfortunate aspect of it all is that all the work that I did with her did not help with the OCD one little bit. It is a shame since that was the reason that I went to her in the first place. The overall fact is that this therapist really helped me, but it did not make any difference at all with my OCD. It is too bad that it was, yet another, failed attempted to free myself from Obsessive Compulsive Disorder.

I now knew that traditional therapy did not work for OCD. I began to look into non-traditional therapy. When you have OCD, you start to look into things more as you feel or, rather hope, that there has to be something that will work. By now,

I had tried so many things but decided to go for one more. I thought about it over and over. I finally decided that I need to try a non-traditional therapy. I thought about hypnosis.

I thought that hypnosis might have a better result. The problem with traditional therapy is that you can only discuss things in your life that you actually remember. I thought that since hypnosis deals with your subconscious, there might be something that I am not conscious of that is causing the OCD. I might have some hidden issue that I do not even know about. Maybe there is an issue from my past that I don't think had an effect on me, but it actually did. I figured that hypnosis would bring that out. I would be able to learn what my subconscious pain was and bring it into my consciousness. That is, if there is any hidden pain. Then I would be able to heal it. This might lower the OCD. Maybe a combination of the two types of therapy would work. I could try to help myself on a subconscious level. We all have things in our past that seemed little as they happened, but the reality is that they were more painful than imagined. A lot of things happen in each of our childhoods that seem to be forgotten. They seem to have slipped by with no effect. This might not be correct. Maybe a part of us is still hurt or suffering from something that we do not even realize was so traumatic. It could be something from our family life or something from school where we were out in the world. It might be with a family member, a friend, a relationship or an event that happened. There might be something that you went through such as dealing with a bully or a family tragedy. Even though these things are long gone and in the past, you might not have dealt with the pain completely. This would mean that you have held onto it. This might cause the stress and OCD on a subconscious level. Maybe it is some current person or event that is an issue that you do not realize. Maybe it is your place in life. Maybe you are secretly afraid of something. Maybe you are secretly angry about something. Maybe you are upset about something in your current life and don't even realize it. Who knows? Hypnosis is worth a try for me. If nothing comes of it, it will not be the first time. Maybe I will find out something big and be able to heal it. Then I can get rid of the OCD forever. The truth is that you never know what the answer might be. It sounds crazy, but you never really know. At this point, I was willing to try anything. Hey, after I tried all of the other things, why not? What is the worst thing that could happen? Nothing? I have had that result before. At least, I will have exhausted one more option.

I am not sure if you know how hypnosis works. I am not sure if they all work in the same way. Here is the process as I understand it. As you know, we do not use our entire brain in life. There is a very large part that is hard to understand and harder to access. This is the subconscious. The subconscious is a neatly wrapped package that is difficult to decipher. We all have one and do not really know that goes on back there. A hypnotist helps you to access this part of your brain. They can help you get back there and see what is really supposedly going on. It is believed that the subconscious can hold the key to what we really feel and how we process our daily life. I am not really sure. I am either going to find out the high level spiritual reason that life and earth exists and my place within that...or...that Sriracha Sauce gives me heartburn. It can go either way. Anyway, hypnosis works differently than traditional therapy. It is much more difficult. It takes some time or a few sessions for you to become comfortable with your therapist and the process. The therapist will help you access your subconscious in order to see what is really going on. This will help you find out what your real issues are. This is where your fear, anger or sadness can be hidden. Then, by finding out that information, you will then consciously know about it. You will bring it into your conscious mind. Once in your conscious mind; this knowledge will enable you to realize it and help yourself to heal those issues. For someone with OCD, this sounds like it might be a good thing. I might have something to deal with. I might be able to heal that part of myself and will be able to get rid of the OCD forever.

The process is interesting. I want to start off by telling you that the theory that a hypnotist can give you a subconscious suggestion that makes you do something weird like moo like a cow is incorrect. I hope! I really doubt I will start loudly meowing every time someone says the word peanut butter or yelling the word ice cream every time my phone rings. Anyway, here is the process: You go into the therapist's office. They put you in a meditative type state and you try to connect with your emotions. You close your eyes and they ask you questions. The questions are on the visuals you might see or emotions you might feel. There is traditional talk therapy before and after. You go into the meditative state by the hypnotist counting you down starting at ten and ending at one. Then, they bring you out of it by counting you up by starting at one and ending with ten. The entire time that you are in the meditative state is where the actual therapy is. It supposedly takes a little while to be able to access any real information. The process also includes voice recordings. These voice recordings are created by the therapist. The therapist will record some of your sessions. They will only record the portion that you are in the meditative state. The therapist will put you into the meditative state. They will give you things to think about in a calm and serene voice. These narratives will get you to think about specific things. They will ask you to visualize things while guiding you. They will guide you to thinking and feeling a certain way. They will tell you what types of things to think about. Then they will bring you out of the meditative state. This entire process will be recorded. They will provide you with the recording. The therapist will tell you when and how often to listen to the recordings in between appointments. Maybe a one or two-week span where you listen to the recording every day. This is designed for you to hear the recording over and over. This repetition will eventually get into your consciousness. Then you will be able to feel or apply the recording to your daily conscious life. An example would be to listen to a recording where you need to realize the things in your life that you are grateful for. By doing this each and every day, you will bring it out of your subconscious and then into your consciousness. You will then be able to see how grateful you are for certain things in your life such as jobs, friends, family, pets and many other things. You get the idea? Basically there are three basic parts of hypnosis. One is traditional talk therapy. Two is a meditative state where you bring up your past or present emotions and feelings in order to bring them into your conscious mind so you are aware of them and can heal them. The third part is the recordings from the meditative state where you can think about all of the positive things in your life and can be thankful for them. Now that I knew all this, I figured I should pick a therapist and begin. I researched a few therapists and chose one. I set up an appointment.

I showed up at my hypnotist's office and sat in one of the empty seats in the waiting room. A few minutes later, one of the doors opened. The hypnotist invited me in. I got up and walked into the office. There was a large massage table, a couch and a chair. She sat in the chair. I sat on the couch. She asked me a few questions about myself. I told her about my family, friends, career issues and, of course, the OCD. She was a very calm woman. There was a definite Zen type quality present. She was a spiritual thinker. She believed that everything was created by your own spirit. I accepted that and we started to get some work done.

She told me to get comfortable on the couch and to relax and close my eyes. I did this and she counted me down from ten to one. I was now, supposedly, under. She, in a calm and relaxed manner and tone, told me to think of a calm and comfortable place. I thought of the calmest and comfortable place that I know...Maui! So, I imagined that I was sitting on the calm and warm beaches of Maui. She had me think of a few positive things. Then, she counted me back up from one to ten. I was now up and awake. I was out of the meditative state. We spent the rest of the session discussing different aspects of my life. It was an odd session compared to traditional talk therapy.

The next couple of sessions were sort of all the same. The topics were all different issues pertaining to my life. My relationships, my friendships, my career choices and my inner child. OK, this was the second time a therapist brought up my inner child as a source for creating the OCD. OK, that's odd! It is interesting that the therapists tell me that it is my inner child that is holding the OCD and keeping it going. Well, let's see what happened as I continued with the hypnotist.

As I mentioned, a lot of the sessions were the same. There were generally two types of sessions. One, we just talked and discussed my life and what I could change. Two, actually using the hypnosis as a healing method. There were two types of hypnosis. One, I would try to communicate with my inner child in order to find out what the actual issue was and why I continued to use the OCD to deal with it. Two, getting into a hypnotic state in order to create a recording that I would continue to listen to. By listening to these recordings, I would get the recording and positive thoughts into the conscious part of my brain. This would, in turn, help me begin to heal.

The sessions now consisted of both talk therapy and some form of hypnosis. I would go into the therapist's office. We would talk for most of the session. At the end of some of the sessions, I would lay back and relax with my eyes closed. She would count me down from ten to one. Then give me some things to think about in terms of my life. These items would be about success, gratitude and overall positive life feelings. I would take deep breaths throughout the process. The therapist would give me subconscious suggestions in order to bring positivity and good thoughts into my life. She always spoke in a calm and relaxed voice. Then, she would count me up from one to ten. Then, I would wake up and feel refreshed. I would be completely out of the hypnotic state. It would be over. I would be back to usual. I would leave the session. Then I would listen to the recordings as much as possible in between each session. She made a lot of recordings.

I believe that the reality of hypnosis is that it is really traditional therapy for your subconscious. It is basically taking your subconscious to therapy. I get the idea.

I went to the hypnotist for over a year. To be honest, I did have some good results. I made a lot of positive changes in my life. I gained success in a few areas. The hypnosis really did help. But there is one part of my life that the hypnosis did not help. Can you guess? Yes, the OCD. The hypnosis did not help with the OCD. I still have it. It did not work the way that I had hoped. So, another failed attempt to free myself from my Obsessive Compulsive Disorder. That's too bad!

There is another thing that I would like to add to this chapter. I have tried many different types of therapy. The problem is that each and every therapist starts off by contradicting all the other therapists that I have been to. I tell them what the other therapists have said and determined. The first thing they all do is contradict them. This brings you to a very confident place, right? Now what? Each of them starts off by telling me that the other person was wrong and that I wasted my time and money trying to help myself with the other person. They are all claiming to be a medical professional. They all have certain licenses. They are all representatives of what the medical community has to offer. They all tell me different things when I begin with them. How am I supposed to trust these people when they all contradict each other with their completely different theories on why I have OCD. They then tell me how they are able to fix it and heal me. It is ridiculous. I have heard so many different theories. Then who is right? Who do you believe? Who has the right answers? You see why the therapy route was difficult? After a few different therapy attempts with no results on the OCD, I began to feel that therapy is not the answer.

My final thoughts about the overall wellness advice is this, NO ONE KNOWS WHAT THEY ARE TALKING ABOUT!!! Everyone will tell you different ideas and theories. Each time you talk to someone, you get your hopes up that this is the one. This is right and this will end the OCD. They will all drone on about their thoughts and theories about life. Keep in mind...none of them actually have Obsessive Compulsive Disorder. This is a major strike against them. The truth is that if none of them actually have and experience a life with OCD; they really DO NOT know what will work. I seriously doubt that their wonderful methods have helped someone with OCD free themselves of it. So, they might help you lose weight and feel better. They might help someone be successful in a career or a relationship. They might have helped many people. This does not mean that they have any idea of how to get rid of or even lessen OCD.

Let's face it, talk is cheap. Sure, they are just trying to help. I get that. It is appreciated. They all tell us things that may help. They don't realize that these so called cures take a tremendous toll on one's life. They do not have to do these things themselves. They do not have to try and find ways to alleviate the symptoms. They do not have to do the things they are telling you to do. Because of this, it does not matter to them how bad their suggestions are, they don't have to live by them. It is much easier to give advice then to have to take it. It is much easier to tell someone how to live than to live like that. It is much easier to tell someone what they need to do and how they need to function without having to function that way for yourself. The point is that we all know first-hand what it is like to live with OCD. And we all just want the same thing...A CURE!!!

CHAPTER 16: THE SPIRITUAL SIDE!

"A Little Woo Woo For You!"

The spiritual side! Obsessive Compulsive Disorder is in the nervous system. Most doctors will tell you that it is a purely physical problem due to the neurons in your brain that are not functioning properly; a low serotonin level, your DNA, etc. which cause the OCD. This is one hundred percent true. It is real and actual. The OCD is inside the body. The brain sends you the irrational thoughts and anxiety. It creates the misleading feelings as well as the uncomfortable situations. It is purely physical and has scientific specifications that bear out its existence.

I have had it long enough to know that there is also a spiritual component to the Obsessive Compulsive Disorder. There is a reason that the OCD raises and lowers. There is a part of you that utilizes the OCD in order to cover your true feelings about something. I believe that this is the spiritual side of the OCD. Perhaps it can be called a coping mechanism. There is a part of you that uses it when needed. This is why it can raise and lower. This may also explain why each individual with OCD has different symptoms and triggers than someone else with the exact same disorder. It will dictate the strength of the OCD as well as the feelings attached. This is a complex system within the body that is a working part of who we are. I believe that no matter what the doctors research dictates; that there is definitely a spiritual side to the Obsessive Compulsive Disorder.

The main thing that no one really discusses is the fact that your emotions play a huge part in the OCD. The OCD will raise and lower depending on how you feel. Any emotion can trigger the OCD. You can be mad, sad, depressed, happy, excited, filled with joy, etc. Either way, these emotions will have an effect of the OCD. Doctors will tell you that when you are stressed out, the OCD will appear worse. They will tell you that when you are mad, it might get worse. I agree with them. I also agree with the fact that when you have an emotion, no matter what it is, the OCD will appear different. If I get mad, the OCD is stronger. If I am sad, the OCD is stronger. I feel this is because there is a part of myself covering my true feelings. Basically, you turn the OCD into busy work. You use it to cover your real emotions so that you do not have to deal with what is really going on. You sort of cover the real emotions with a blanket of OCD. This way, you are consciously "busy" and do not have the time to look at what is really going on in your life to cause this OCD.

The OCD could possibly be a sort of coping mechanism that you use when necessary. You use it conveniently. You use it when it suits you. You use it as a means to distract you from yourself. You use it to negate your true emotions. Basically, why deal with the fact that something made you feel a certain way when you can do a compulsion to cover it up. An example would be that you will not admit that you are afraid of going on a trip so you just check the refrigerator twenty-five times. Why admit that someone made a comment that made you mad when you can repeat twelve times. Why deal with the fact that you are afraid when you can walk in and out of a room ten times. You see what I mean? It very well can be a coping mechanism. You use it when you have an emotion that you want to cover up. What is currently going on in your life will dictate how bad the OCD will become. It is how people like me deal with their everyday life.

Take me for example, when I am afraid of something, my OCD skyrockets. When I am nervous, it skyrockets. If I am mad, it skyrockets. On the other hand, If I am happy, relaxed or ex-cited, the OCD is very low. It depends on my reaction to whatever is going on in my life at the time. There are always times where a person will get nervous and stressed out about something. This is just life. Life is stressful for everyone at times. The difference is that someone with OCD will react to the stress with the OCD. It will become worse and worse depending on the amount of stress that they have in their life. We all know that stress carries tremendous impact. It can affect the mental and physical aspects of someone's life. If you have OCD, this is how the stress will affect you. The OCD becomes stronger and more detailed. It lasts longer and longer. The symptoms get worse and worse. The compulsions get more demanding. The thoughts will explode. It is just a way of life.

Your emotions and feelings dictate the level of complexity. If you are going through a bad time in your life, the OCD will get worse. If you are going through a good time in your life, you may just be left with the force of habit compulsions that you usually have. They are usually very manageable. When you are upset, you might experience some new symptoms that you have never had before. You might develop new versions of your old symptoms or different ways of doing the compulsions. You might experience new thoughts and new feelings. It all depends on your emotions.

The reality is that some of the OCD depends on YOU! If you are worried about something, then you will trigger the OCD so that you feel more comfortable. This is the basic idea that you sort of hide inside of your own OCD symptoms. The OCD symptoms will cover up the fact that you are worried. There is a part of you that is encouraging this OCD storm to exist. Basically, you are trying to distract yourself from yourself and what is really going on. You are hiding your true emotions.

I think this is due to the force of habit. You basically have developed this intricate system to cover your real emotions. You have been unconsciously creating this for many years. So, it is just what you do. It is the way that you deal with life. You get used to it at a young age and then you feel comfortable doing it. Then, it is just the way that you deal with things. Like I said, it is a coping mechanism. This mechanism suits you and you use it. It is your "Go To" reaction to the life around you. No matter what is going on in your life, you will deal with it this way.

The OCD becomes a way of life. It is a band aid to cover up the real issues. The force of habit, the obsessions, the compulsions and the anxiety. It is a way that you "Deal" with things that come up in your daily life. It is your defense mechanism. It is an intricate system designed to make you look the other way. Instead of admitting that you are nervous about a first date, you will just check the front door fifty times. Instead of admitting that you are nervous about a dinner party, you will just check the bathroom faucet twenty times. Instead of admitting that you are angry about what someone said, you will check the oven thirty times. You see how it works? Now let's look at a few examples of situations that might raise the OCD.

My example is with me checking a friend's house. My friend was out of town. I went to her house to check on the place and get her mail. I did what I needed to do. I then left the house and it was time to lock the door. I immediately had the obsession that I did not lock the door. I then got the fear that the door is open and all of her belongings will be stolen. Then, the OCD kicks in and I am checking the front door. Notice, the real emotion is fear that I screwed something up that would harm our friendship. The OCD then covered it up with the checking of the front door in sets. See how the true emotions affect the OCD?

The above example is of a smaller emotion. There are larger emotions that will affect the OCD in a much bigger way. You might be afraid to grow up, move to a different state, get a new job, get a divorce, get married, have a child, deal with the death of a parent or loved one or some other major life change. I gave an example of the smaller and sort of day to day example. You might have the usually light emotions or a much deeper seeded emotion that is causing you to trigger your OCD. There might be some sort of pain or trauma that you never faced and dealt with. This might be a major event in your life that had a deeper effect than you had thought. This might be a painful time that you went through and you never really dealt with the emotions that followed. It might deal with loss, fear, anger, etc. Only you know what that cause is. It might be completely subconscious. Either way, it will have an effect on the OCD. We all have good times in life as well as bad. It is referred to as the ups and downs of life. The stronger the emotions are, the worse the OCD will be.

My OCD gets worse during these emotional times. I tend to get higher OCD when I am getting ready for a date. The real reason that the OCD is worse is due to the fact that I am worried about the date. Meeting someone new. I want the date to go well. Will they like me? Will I like them?

I might have a dinner party to go to with a bunch of people that I do not know. This will raise the OCD due to the fact that I want the night to be enjoyable. I will need to be on my best behavior and will need to watch the things that I say and do. The real issue is that I am nervous as to how the night will turn out.

I might have a dental appointment. I am nervous about the appointment and what the dentist will tell me or do to me. The OCD will rise to the occasion.

I might have higher OCD prior to a trip. The real issue is that I am nervous about the fact that I am getting on a plane. I am nervous about our safety so the OCD will reflect that. I might check the front door longer due to the fact that I will not be there for a while and something could happen to my home. I might check my luggage more times because I am nervous that I will forget something that I need to bring like my license, passport or any medications.

In conclusion, no matter what happens in your life, it will affect the OCD. The OCD will be there in all aspects of your life. Whether it is a good time or bad time, the OCD will be there. It is just something that someone like me has to deal with. I just know that the OCD is reacting to how I feel and what I am going through at that particular time. I am used to it. I know it will happen. I know that it is caused by my emotions. The truth is that my emotions will always have an effect on my life. Period. See how that works?

CHAPTER 17: DEDICATION!

"To The Ones Who Love Us!"

Dedication! You hear the term dedication a lot. Celebrities dedicate their awards to people that have helped them get to where they are. People dedicate buildings and other things to all the people that made their project happen. People give dedication speeches for a lot of different things.

This chapter is a dedication to all of the people in our lives. All of the people in the lives of someone with Obsessive Compulsive Disorder. All of the people who are there for us. Who help us. Who care for us. Who love us. Who want us to get better. Who are there for us to talk to. Who are there to listen to our pain. Who are there to help us in any way that they can. Who will listen to our stories, trials and tribulations. These are the people in our lives. They are our Mothers, Fathers, Sisters, Brothers, Spouses and Friends. Basically, anyone who is there for us every step of the way.

Think of the commitment that they have made to us just by always being there. They do not have OCD. They do not have obsessions, compulsions, anxiety, weird thoughts, weird feelings, or anything else that goes with the OCD lifestyle. They do not have to live the OCD lifestyle at all...but they do. They end up repeating with us, checking with us, assisting with all thoughts and compulsions. They end up consoling us when we are in the midst of an OCD issue. They are sad when we are sad and celebrate when we are happy.

They spend a lot of their lives living with OCD even when they do not even have it. They learn all of the medical aspects, physical aspects and emotional aspects. They are right there with us when we go to a new neurologist. They are there when we start a new medication. They are there for us no matter what.

The people in our lives tolerate the repeating with us because they know it makes us feel better and relieves the anxiety. They do whatever it takes to help us. They research all of the new treatments out there as well as keep tabs on the old ones. They give us feedback as to how they think that we are doing. They make us feel a ray of hope when we are at our lowest moment. They acknowledge us when we are doing well and console us when we are not doing as well. They watch us through our suffering and pain. They celebrate our wins with us.

Obsessive Compulsive Disorder! They don't have it. Yet, they have to learn the life of someone with Obsessive Compulsive Disorder. This is a lifelong support of another human being. You've got to give them so much credit for that. They help us through our lives. They help us navigate through the good and the bad moments. They help us lift our head high when we are not in a good place. They really give up a lot of their life to serve ours. These are the people that deserve some recognition. I know this is only a small chapter but it has a big message. I just want to communicate how much these people mean to us and to say one big...THANK YOU FOR LOVING US UNCONDITIONALLY!

CHAPTER 18: ACCEPTANCE!

"Whatever...Screw It!"

Acceptance! A lot of people use the term acceptance for many different situations. A lot of people use the sentence "You have to accept the fact that...". This sentence is usually used when something did not end the way it was supposed to. Acceptance can be used to comfort someone if they are sad or angry about something in their life. Acceptance can also be used to support someone when they could not create a desired outcome. Maybe a relationship or marriage did not work out. Maybe they did not get the job that they really wanted. Maybe they lost someone close to them. There are many different reasons that people throw the term "You need to accept it!" around. That is probably how the term, "Shit Happens!" came to be. As we all know, it does!

There are some people who believe that the act of acceptance is a spiritual ability. There are some people that just believe that you accept things. No matter what you believe in, what religion you are part of, or what your views on life are...acceptance will be a part of your life. It is inevitable. We all accept the things in our lives in different ways. You do not have to be an enlightened Tibetan monk to be able to accept the things that come your way. You do not need to be fanatic about your yoga master. You also do not need to be the type of person that believes in a higher form of universal presence that knows all. You do not need to be spiritual in any way and believe that there is some greater good or reason for everything. You just need to be human and the acceptance is already there.

It can be devastatingly painful to live with Obsessive Compulsive Disorder. I have tried many different things to get rid of the OCD. I have tried things to lower it and tried things to get rid of it completely. I was hopeful with each and everything that I have done. I really tried and hoped for a different solution. The reality is that everything that I have done ended up the same way...I have Obsessive Compulsive Disorder. No matter what I tried or how weird that it was; it was all the same result...I still have OCD. I tried various methods of relaxation, spirituality, medication, homeopathic/natural remedies, physical remedies and still...I have OCD.

Obsessive Compulsive Disorder is a lifelong burden. It is just the way that I need to live. It is the overall huge part of my life. It is a major piece of the puzzle that makes up me. It is intertwined in everything that I do, say and feel. It is difficult to deal with. It is very hard to live with.

The reality is that I need to do one final thing...ACCEPT IT! I need to just accept the fact that I will always have OCD. Nothing will fix it or take it away. I will always live this way and will always need to manage it. This is, to say the least...my life. I accept it. I understand it. I need to be OK with it. It is just who I am.

ABOUT THE AUTHOR

Jeffrey Benson

Jeffrey Benson has lived with OCD since he was a little boy. He had to struggle to cope with this disorder. In doing so, he learned how to manage the iterations of this disorder and actively live his life. At this point in time, he is at acceptance for the man that he is.

PRAISE FOR AUTHOR

"Jeffrey's book "Locked In Numbers" is an intimate glimpse into what it's like to live with obsessive compulsive disorder. It chronicles the various manifestations of this complex disorder and describes Jeffrey's search for an enduring solution. "Locked In Numbers" is a must read for anyone who wishes to understand OCD and, more importantly, it provides hope for those who suffer from the condition. Highly recommended."

- MICHAEL LARA, M.D.

www.ingramcontent.com/pod-product-compliance
Lightning Source LLC
Chambersburg PA
CBHW060021100426
42740CB00010B/1552